TRUE LOVE

The Grace of Christian Fellowship

A Confessional Perspective

TRUE LOVE

The Grace of Christian Fellowship

A Confessional Perspective

James M. Renihan

Broken Wharfe

TRUE LOVE

The Grace of Christian Fellowship

A Confessional Perspective

First published as *True Love: Understanding the real meaning of Christian love* by EP in 2010.

ISBN 978-1-7393653-6-3

Broken Wharfe

This book was edited by Broken Wharfe.

Typeset in Adobe Garamond Pro by Jill Sawyer Phypers
Printed in the UK by TJ Books Ltd, Padstow, Cornwall
Cover art: © Jude May Design
www.judemaydesign.com
Cover images © channarongsds | iStock

brokenwharfe.com

James Renihan warmly and ably opens up the great subject of love in 1 Corinthians 13. He challenges our self-centredness and urges us to pursue true love—a love which is founded in God's prior love and is to permeate and motivate every aspect of the Christian's life.

Robert Strivens
Pastor, Bradford on Avon Baptist Church, Wiltshire, UK
Former Principal, London Seminary

This is one of the best books I've read for a long time. James Renihan has done us a great service. How should you read this book? In small parts, meditating prayerfully on each portion (the chapter subheadings are ideal for this). *True Love*'s usefulness is enhanced because the author first sets these verses within the context of the whole letter of 1 Corinthians, and then shows why they sit between Paul's two chapters dealing with spiritual gifts.

Walter Johnston
Actively retired and former Pastor for 27 years, Chorlton Evangelical Church, Manchester, UK

The part that most people seem to like about Christianity is love. How many times have you heard 1 Corinthians 13 read at weddings? Yet love is gravely misunderstood in our culture, apart from the wider scope of God's character, commands, and saving work in Christ. James Renihan deserves our gratitude because he neither sentimentalizes nor intellectualizes love. Here is a rich, vivid, and concrete exploration of this fantastic subject.

Michael Horton
Ordained minister, United Reformed Churches in North America
Professor of Systematic Theology & Apologetics, Westminster Seminary, California

In *True Love*, James Renihan puts 1 Corinthians 13 firmly in its context. Beginning with God's love for us in Christ, and the law and gospel of love, Renihan also situates chapter 13 in the epistle as a whole and then—without dealing with other contentious issues—focuses on this love, its importance, and its outworking. Given how misunderstood and abused the whole notion of love is both within and without the church, and how often abused and sentimentalized this chapter can be, this is a powerful corrective to shallow and errant views, providing us with a solid, careful, and challenging study of this most vital Christian grace and duty.

Jeremy Walker
Pastor, Maidenbower Baptist Church, Crawley, UK

If you're looking for a short and sweet book that discusses the famous "love" chapter in the Bible, you'll want to get *True Love* by Dr. James Renihan. I'd recommend this book for anyone studying 1 Corinthians or the biblical theme of love. I'd also recommend this book as a good one to read/discuss in your church's community group, book club, or Bible study—from high school to older adult, both men and women. Finally, it would make a great gift book—not too long and tedious, but short, sweet, and focused on Jesus.

Shane Lems
Minister, Covenant Presbyterian Church OPC, Wisconsin, USA

To Lynne my true love

Contents

Preface

This little book has been a long time in the making. The subject first came to light as a series of sermons and has been preached in various forms at churches and conferences for several years. Every time that I have delivered this material, people have expressed their appreciation of the importance of the topic. This has given me hope that perhaps it will be useful in written form.

Christian love is central to the life of every believer. When Paul speaks of the work of the Holy Spirit in Jesus' followers, love is the first item he mentions (Gal. 5:22); when our Saviour prepared his disciples for the events of that final night in Jerusalem, and everything that would come after, he spoke to them about love (John 13:34–35). Perhaps it is not an overstatement to say that love is at the root of the Christian faith—it is God's abiding and everlasting love that gives impetus to the incarnation of Christ and the redemption of his people.

At first glance, it is surprising that there is so little literature available about love. There may be different reasons for this. While the topic is very important, it is also difficult. Love is not easily defined. In some ways, it is simpler to experience love than to characterize it. Similarly, no author should think that he or she adequately understands, and especially expresses, love. When we ask ourselves questions such as "Am I qualified to write to others about love?" we recognize how far short of the standard we come. We are all striving after a better expression of this grace. As an author, I have to struggle with my failure to achieve the touchstone of which I write. I am sure that others have wrestled with the same difficulty. I hope that, despite my own weakness, God's Spirit has assisted me in writing truthfully and helpfully in this book.

While this work is largely an exposition of 1 Corinthians 13, it is not intended to be a thorough explanation of that chapter. Rather, it is more narrowly focused, an attempt to say something about love as it is found there. Some readers will notice that I have not addressed questions such as the detailed nature of the second coming of our Lord Jesus Christ, or taken a position on the present employment of the gifts of the Spirit (though of course I have very decided views on both of these topics!). A more complete exposition would have investigated them—but doing so is outside of my purpose. Since this material first came to light as a series of sermons about love in 1 Corinthians 13, it has seemed good to follow that path rather than expand the spotlight to include other matters.

Thank you for your interest in this book. I pray that these words will be helpful to you, and that the Lord Jesus will be glorified in your life.

Soli Deo Gloria.

James M. Renihan
President, IRBS Theological Seminary
Mansfield, TX

Chapter 1
AN IMPORTANT PLACE TO BEGIN

We love Him because He first loved us.
1 John 4:19

"How do I love thee? Let me count the ways."

Probably everyone recognizes these familiar words from the pen of Elizabeth Barrett Browning. The poet, in attempting to describe the depths of love, cannot probe its foundations; even an enumeration ("let me count…") is only a poor reflection of reality. A list is only a summary—it has no pulsing beat of life. But these words, and the flowing expressions of the rest of her song, resonate with our own experiences, for they echo our own desires and emotions. We know something of the profound effect true love has on human life.

But we must not have a purely romanticized view of love. When we go beyond the power of feelings, we begin to see that love is hard work and requires much from us. The temporary high provided by romantic attraction does not and cannot sustain the long-term commitment necessary in true love. A simple glance at pop culture with all of its focus on passing emotion proves the point: pleasant and even powerful sensation is not love. It may be a part, but it is far from the whole. Love is far more profound. In fact, we must consider it in a completely different way—we must think of it in terms of the law and, even more importantly, in terms of the gospel.

Love and the Law

From one important perspective, we must recognize that *love is law*. While this phrase may not seem to make sense at first, it is nonetheless true. If you think about it carefully, you will remember that throughout the Bible, love is presented to us as a *commandment*. For example, the foundational requirement for true religion in both Old and New Testaments is this: "love the Lord your God" (Deut. 6:5). When the Jewish mother held her little child on her lap, this was the first principle she taught her, serving as the basis for every aspect of her life. The Lord commanded his people to love him with all of their being. Jesus acknowledged the same principle. When he was confronted by a lawyer from the sect of the Pharisees, and was asked the question, "Which is the great commandment in the law?", he replied by citing Deuteronomy 6:5, calling it the "first and great commandment". Then, he added a second, "love your neighbour as yourself" (Matt. 22:36–40). Just before he faced his trial and crucifixion, as he prepared his disciples for those events while in the Upper Room, he said, "A new commandment I give to you, that you love one another" (John 13:34). Throughout the Bible, we find that love is a precept to be obeyed.

As I have preached on 1 Corinthians 13, this principle has been obvious to me. It is a chapter urging people to love, yet it often produces deep conviction in us because we fall so far short of its lofty standard. We are slain by the law of love. This can be tremendously discouraging. It becomes easy to reason like this: "While I want with all of my heart to grow in this grace, all that I learn tells me that I am far short of meeting its demands. And yet Paul sets it before me as an obligation. What am I to do?" This is an important question, which must be given consideration.

Love and the Gospel

The answer rests in the full testimony of Scripture—its teaching about growth in grace, frequently called the doctrine of *sanctification*. Not only does the Lord give the new birth to his children, but like a good parent, he nurtures them, providing for their progress to maturity. His care is far better than any human father, his love more profound than the most tender mother on earth. When we consider the process he uses to promote this advance, we find the solution to our dilemma. A fundamental principle of growth in grace throughout the Word of God is this: the work of God for us produces the increase of grace in us. Notice the God-centred priority.

Several passages come to mind immediately. For example, when Paul tells the Philippian Christians to "work out your own salvation with fear and trembling" (Phil. 2:12), he immediately adds, "for it is God who works in you both to will and to do for His good pleasure" (2:13). While the Philippians must work, their work is based on the priority of God's activity. In Romans 8:13, the apostle says, "For if you live according to the flesh you will die; but if by the Spirit you put to death the deeds of the body, you will live." In this case, he speaks in terms of life and death. Those who live for the flesh prove by their actions that grace is not at work in them, and those who live in the Spirit truly live, putting to death the sins of the flesh. But who does this? Is it the believer, or is it the Spirit? The text says both. It is not the believer alone, using all of his strength to fight and kill the flesh; nor is it the Spirit alone, acting upon a passive believer. The text says, "by the Spirit you…" Similarly, when Paul speaks of the fruit of the Spirit in Galatians 5:22–23, it is evident that the Spirit brings forth fruit in the life of the believer. But once again, this is not an act upon a motionless subject. Perhaps this is most obvious in the final fruit listed, self-control. Think about this: the fruit of the *Spirit* is *self*-control. Who does this? Obviously, it is the believer, in dependence on the Spirit. I must control myself, but I cannot and will not do it without the Spirit. The same is true for the first fruit in Paul's list, namely love. I must, by the Spirit, love. Only his holy influence will produce this beautiful fruit, but he will only do it as I seek to love.

Sinclair Ferguson has expressed this principle well when he said,

> Sanctification is … the consistent practical outworking of what it means to belong to the new creation in Christ. That is why so much of the New Testament's response to pastoral and personal problems in the early church was: "Do you not know what is true of you in Christ? … Live by the Spirit's power in a manner consistent with that!"[1]

Dr Ferguson simply summarizes the doctrine taught in the great Confessions of the Reformation churches. Notice, for example, how this is expressed in the *Second London Confession* (often called the *1689 Baptist Confession*). In words almost identical to the *Westminster Confession of Faith*, the Baptist document states in chapter 13, entitled "Of Sanctification",

1. They who are united to Christ, Effectually called, and regenerated, having a new heart, and a new Spirit created in them, through the virtue of Christ's death, and Resurrection; are also farther sanctified, really, and personally, through the same virtue, by his

[1] Sinclair Ferguson, "The Reformed View" in *Christian Spirituality: Five Views of Sanctification,* ed. Donald L. Alexander (Downers Grove: InterVarsity, 1988), 60.

word and Spirit dwelling in them; the dominion of the whole body of sin is destroyed, and the several lusts thereof, are more and more weakened, and mortified; and they are more and more quickened, and strengthened in all saving graces, to the practice of all true holiness, without which no man shall see the Lord.

2. This Sanctification is throughout, in the whole man, yet imperfect in this life; there abideth still some remnants of corruption in every part, whence ariseth a continual, and irreconcilable war; the Flesh lusting against the Spirit, and the Spirit against the Flesh.
3. In which war, although the remaining corruption for a time may much prevail; yet through the continual supply of strength from the sanctifying Spirit of Christ the regenerate part doth overcome; and so the Saints grow in Grace, perfecting holiness in the fear of God, pressing after an heavenly life, in Evangelical Obedience to all the commands which Christ as Head and King, in his Word hath prescribed to them.

The Confession is exactly right. It recognizes that the beginning and root of our growth in grace must be found in the work of God in Christ, but we must be active in the pursuit of grace. The picture of warfare is especially powerful. Victories are often won, not simply by virtue of the strength of the army, but by the continuous presence of supplies. Soldiers without food and drink seldom conquer; believers must receive the "continual supply of strength from the sanctifying Spirit of Christ".

The Source of our Love

When I visit churches and have the opportunity to preach, I often choose to proclaim the truth of 1 John 4:19: "We love Him[2] because He first loved us." These eight simple words summarize the doctrine we have briefly described above. They emphasize two simple truths: God loves us; and our love grows from his love for us. In the original language, this is especially evident, for John employs personal pronouns to focus our attention on the personal nature of this love.

Let us consider this verse, but in reverse order. The second part of the text, as written in the sentence, is supplemental to the earlier part (a subordinate clause). Yet in theological terms, it is by far the more basic of the two parts. The very presence of the word "because" demonstrates this. John's assertion in the first statement ("we love Him") depends upon the second ("because He first loved us"). Our action only comes as a result of his prior action.

Sometimes it is easy for us to read quickly over a text, and not contemplate the full beauty of its words. I suspect that sometimes that is the case with a brief verse such as this one. For example, in our text, the individuals are not even named; we find pronouns — *we, him, he, us*. These could be impersonal, but that is as far away from the intent of the apostle as can be imagined. We must identify the persons involved here.

The obvious referent of "he" and "him" is God himself. He loved us. But who is he? Our minds, filled with the teaching of the Word of God, quickly answer this question. He is the high and holy one who

[2] Throughout this book, I have used the New King James Version of the English Bible. Some readers will note that its translation of this verse adds a word ("Him") which is not included in most manuscripts of the Greek New Testament. A more literal rendering of the verse might be, "We love, because he first loved us." The NKJV rendering narrows the focus of the thought slightly. It is right to recognize that true love begins with God and our love for him (the first great commandment) but must also include our love for people (the second great commandment, which according to Jesus is "like it", Matthew 22:39). I have tried to write with this broader idea in view: God's love stimulates our love, first for him, and then for others.

inhabits eternity, living outside of the world in the splendour of his own glory. He is independent and self-sufficient, in need of no one and nothing to satisfy any lack. In majesty and glory, he is unequalled; everything that he has made owes him constant worship. There is no limit to his power, or his wisdom; there is no one able to overcome him, nor does he need an instructor. He is the creator of all things; one who spoke a word, and the universe came into existence. He upholds, or sustains, all things; without his constant attention, they would fall into nothingness. His angelic attendants cry out unceasingly, "Holy, holy, holy, Lord God Almighty, Who was, and is and is to come" (Rev. 4:8). This is the God John presents to us.

It is important for us to notice also that he loves *us*. This clearly refers to believers, and we must pause to think about ourselves. If God is great and glorious, full of power and dominion and holiness, a few moments' thought will remind us that we are the exact opposite. We are his creatures, the work of his power. That alone speaks volumes about our obligation to him. But we are now, after the Fall, not simply creatures, but sinful creatures, dead in our unbelief, wayward, and full of gross wickedness. Morally, we could not be further from his holy perfection. And yet, John asserts that he loves *us*. Why?

In reality, there is only one possible reason, found in 1 John 4:16—God is love. As the apostle speaks about God, he wants us to understand that love is of the very nature of God. Certainly, this is balanced by all of the other attributes: his wisdom, power, holiness, justice, goodness and truth. Nonetheless, love is always present and real.

Occasionally the Bible gives us a glimpse into this wonderful divine love. In John 17:23–25 we read Jesus' prayer,

> "...that the world may know that You have sent Me, and have loved them as You have loved Me.

> "Father, I desire that they also whom You gave Me may be with Me where I am, that they may behold My glory which You have given Me; for You loved Me before the foundation of the world. O righteous Father! The world has not known You, but I have known You; and these have known that You sent Me."

Here the Lord Jesus Christ, as he prays for his people, speaks of the wonderful, eternal, deep and abiding love between the members of the Trinity. This mutual affection is the basis for all other loves, and Jesus wants his people to know this. God is love in his being, and when he chooses to express that love, it is so great that it even breaks through to the worst of his enemies, sinful men and women like me and you.

Now this love of God comes first. Notice that John uses language expressing its primacy: he *first* loved us. Before any other love, God is love—the source and origin of all loves. The eternal mutual love of the Trinity is expressed toward humans, enabling and energizing our love. We ought to be astounded at this truth! The great triune God of heaven and earth, all-powerful, all-wise, all-glorious, loves *you* with a perfect, everlasting unquenchable love.

The expression of our love

As we contemplate this fact, we realize that our love grows out of his love for us. God's love alone causes our love to grow and develop. We can look at 1 John 4:10: "In this is love, not that we loved God, but that He loved us and sent His Son to be the propitiation for our sins." It is not unlike Romans 5:8: "God demonstrates His own love toward us, in that while we were still sinners, Christ died for us." The only reason that we are able to love is that he loved first. It has been said,

"Our love is the light kindled by the love of God."[3] Certainly this is right. Our adoration for God is the fruit growing in the soil of his love for us.

Primarily, we are speaking here about personal affection. We must not confuse love with its fruits: duty, worship, service, doctrine etc. John is speaking about personal relationships, and the attachments that come with them. He is describing the response that a believer gives to this great Object of affection, which is foundational to all true duty, worship, service and doctrine. It is the believer's attachment to God, the recognition of his loveliness and desirability, that is presented here. This is the heart of the issue—God is to be desired, to be loved with great fervour, simply for who he is. In his essence, he is wonderful and full of love, and our response is to return love for loveliness.

The increase of our love is found here. John would have us contemplate God and his love, bathing in the inexhaustible depths of his grace and mercy. As we do this, our love is nurtured and nourished, resulting in beautiful fruit. Do you ever contemplate God's love for you, personally? Do you ever think about the fact that he delights in you? Christian, this is your God! He loves you with an overwhelming, undying, unquenchable love; you personally—the God of the universe loves you.

Does that make you love him? It should. Puritan writer Thomas Watson said, "Love makes the duties of religion pleasant."[4] Do you sometimes find that the duties of Christianity become dry and dull? Meditate on God's love, and who he is, and you will soon find a change in your life. A God-centred life, full of the gospel, is the basis

---

[3] B. F. Westcott, *The Epistles of St John: The Greek Text with Notes and Essays* (Grand Rapids: Eerdmans, 1966), 161.

[4] Thomas Watson, quoted in Robert Aitkin Bertram, ed., *A Homiletic Encyclopaedia of Illustrations in Theology and Morals* (New York: Funk & Wagnalls, 1889), 559.

for all that we do.

It really does no good to contemplate the duties, the laws, of the Bible, and then determine to do them in your own strength. That is the certain recipe for frustration. With love, and our lack of it, we will not grow simply by gritting our teeth, clenching our fists, and deciding that we will love, whatever it takes! No, not at all. We must look to heaven, contemplate Christ and depend on his Spirit. Then we will grow.

Love *is* a commandment. But, like every other commandment, it is law to be obeyed by the empowerment of God's gracious Holy Spirit. As you read these pages, do not despair. You will find yourself falling short of the fulness of true love over and over. You will wonder if you will ever be able to show the kind of love described by the apostle. Remember what we have said. Your love will flow from God's love. Walk in the Spirit, and you will see this grace develop in your life. May God help us increase in love, as we gaze on his love for us.

Chapter 2
A WAY THAT IS BEYOND COMPARISON

And yet I show you a more excellent way... Pursue love...
1 Corinthians 12:31; 14:1

Of all the poems, sonnets, and stories in praise of love, 1 Corinthians 13 shines brightest. In a few simple words, the essence of this joyous emotion is presented to our understandings. We must learn from it, following its path, rejoicing in its joys, seeking its treasure.

When one reads Paul's first letter to the church at Corinth, it becomes obvious that they were an assembly beset by troubles. From the very first paragraphs, there are signs of sin, weakness and deficiency in this congregation. Our chapter comes in the midst of Paul seeking to address these troubles. In order to understand properly our text, we must view it as part of the whole letter. By itself, it is sublimely beautiful and meaningful. But when cast into the flow of thought of the entire epistle, it is even more impressive. It is Paul's bare-heart attempt to confront and solve the Corinthian problems. To him, love is life, the climate in which all must be done, the centre of the remedy for their troubles. Love, pure and simple, as described in the verses before us. We need to see how Paul's doctrine of love in chapter 13 addresses and answers the problems of the Corinthian

Christians. When writing his beautiful song, the apostle never thinks of it in isolation. It is not simply a moving description of a lofty ideal; rather, it is the remedy for the deep difficulties afflicting the church.

The First Epistle to the Corinthians

First, let us examine Paul's relationship with the Corinthian church. In Acts 18, Luke, Paul's frequent travelling companion, tells us that the apostle was responsible, under God, for the founding of the church in Corinth. This was probably four or five years prior to the writing of this epistle. While we are not told the exact length of his stay in that city, it was longer than eighteen months, in which he was actively involved in "teaching the word of God among them" (Acts 18:11). Certainly, this was a period in which much good would have been accomplished for the kingdom of God. Relationships would have been built, believers established in the things of the Lord, and leaders trained for the work of the ministry. It was not, however, a time of unceasing blessing. Much opposition arose, especially from the Jews, culminating in Paul's departure to Syria. After leaving Corinth, he apparently maintained contact and communication with the church and its members. 1 Corinthians 5:9 clearly tells us that there was an earlier epistle sent by Paul to the church. In 1 Corinthians 1:11, a personal report, given to Paul by 'those of Chloe's household", informed him of some of the troubles in the assembly, and it seems that Stephanas, Fortunatus and Achaicus had likewise visited the apostle with news (16:17). 1 Corinthians 7:1 demonstrates that the Corinthians themselves had also written a letter, to Paul, seeking his advice on a variety of matters. Evidently, there was regular contact between the apostle and these believers.

In many ways, the report from Chloe's people and the letter sent to Paul by the Corinthians structure the contents of this letter, known to us as 1 Corinthians. Chapters 1–6 seem to deal with matters arising from the report, and chapters 7–16 answer the issues contained in the church's letter. But there is also an underlying theme running through the entire letter, a theme that seems to be at the root of the Corinthian problem: an overestimation of themselves and of their position. As a result of what God had done with them, perhaps augmented with pride in their geographic location as inhabitants of a very important trading centre, they developed a sinful pride of position which blinded them to several key realities of Christian life and doctrine.

Surpassing Grace

Let's notice some of these things in the body of the epistle itself. Almost the first thing that Paul writes to them is this:

> I thank my God always concerning you for the grace of God which was given to you by Christ Jesus, that you were enriched in everything by Him in all utterance and all knowledge, even as the testimony of Christ was confirmed in you, so that you come short in no gift, eagerly waiting for the revelation of our Lord Jesus Christ, who will also confirm you to the end, that you may be blameless in the day of our Lord Jesus Christ. (1 Cor. 1:4–8)

It is evident from these words that both Paul and the Corinthians recognized that the Lord had done something extraordinary in their midst. The grace of God had been active throughout the many months that Paul was present, and afterwards as well, so much so that the apostle could speak of the abundance of riches given to them by Christ himself. The emphasis of 1:5 is on the source of the riches: they have come from the blessing of Christ. This is not the wealth of jewels and gold, but rather of spiritual blessings, divinely granted. Two categories are especially named: speech and knowledge, each highly valued in Greek culture. Of course, the rest of the chapter demonstrates that Paul is not thinking in the worldly categories of the pagan philosophers, but rather in spiritual terms of the cross and its wisdom. Contrary to the false knowledge and oratory prevalent among the Greeks, the Corinthians had experienced a divine enrichment of sound speech and spiritual knowledge.

Beyond this, they also "came short in no gift". This is a figure of speech indicating that there was no other church that had been blessed with such a varied and extensive distribution of supernatural gifts. Apparently, every divine manifestation intended for use by the Christian church had been present among the Corinthian believers. They could rejoice, as did Paul, in this amazing distribution by the ascended Lord. He had determined to bless this church to the fullest, and they had experienced and enjoyed this overflow of heavenly grace. But not all was well. In spite of these enormous blessings, trouble was in their midst.

Surpassing Pride

This great abundance of blessings became the cause of their pride. This thread runs throughout the epistle. After addressing the problem of division, Paul turns to the problem of the Corinthian boasting in chapter 4. It seems that some members of the church had attached themselves to one or another of the apostles, as if belonging to some kind of "party" of another was a cause for personal pride. If it was wrong for even the apostles to think in these man-centred terms (as party attachment centres on men), how much more true is this of all believers? God alone is the one who acts in and through Christians.

Consider Paul's words:

> For who makes you differ from another? And what do you have that you did not receive? Now if you did indeed receive it, why do you boast as if you had not received it? You are already full! You are already rich! You have reigned as kings without us—and indeed I could wish you did reign, that we also might reign with you! (1 Cor. 4:7-8)

These folks were clearly convinced of their own inflated status. This series of questions was intended by Paul to serve as a means of contemplation and conviction. If one excels over another in gifts, who causes this? Isn't it the Lord? And is there anything that they received that did not come from his hand? And if this is the case, why did they boast? They had taken their eyes off the Lord, and firmly placed them on themselves. The man who exercised the more spectacular gift took pride in what he had done, forgetting that it was the Lord working through him. Christ might have just as sovereignly determined to use another individual to do the same thing. But this truth was lost on the Corinthians, and they boasted of their (spiritual) wealth. They were kings—not servants of the true King, but kings in their own right. They had completely missed the point.

A few verses later, Paul addressed the problem of the Corinthians' "puffed up" demeanour. They were puffed up by their independence from the apostle (1 Cor. 4:18–19); they were puffed up by their tolerance toward gross sin in their midst (5:2); they were puffed up by their liberty (8:9). So out of proportion was their sense of self-importance that they seem to have adopted a slogan for themselves: "All things are lawful" (6:12; 10:23). When an individual thinks that he or she is superior, even when that perceived superiority comes from God, all boundaries are lost. One may begin to excuse even the worst of sinful acts, thinking that the experience of superlative blessings somehow brings oneself into a heavenly sphere. Sadly, the Corinthians fell right into this trap.

It perhaps should not be a surprise that the pride present among the Corinthians fomented a party spirit among them. Pride is not merely an intellectual problem. When it gets a grip in the heart, it is not content merely to nurse its own inflated sense of greatness, but it wants others to recognize it. This is evident in the disintegration of unity in this assembly. Immediately after thanking God for the wonderful blessings that he had poured out on the church, the apostle addressed a fundamental problem among them: divisions. There is an unmistakable connection between pride and division.

Paul's words in 1 Corinthians 10:12 directly address this situation: "let him who thinks he stands take heed lest he fall." This was the great problem of the Corinthians. So far as they were concerned, all of their blessings were unshakable evidence that they indeed stood firm in their faith. But in fact, they were on the verge of falling, because in relying on themselves and their experiences, they had lost touch with Christ. Self-absorption, self-congratulation, self-confidence, were the carnal factors at the root of the Corinthian problem.

It is especially fascinating to notice that their pride was evident in the two areas mentioned by Paul in his introductory statement, namely wisdom and spiritual gifts. Notice, for example, that Paul speaks of the difference between worldly wisdom and divine wisdom as the theme of the first extended section of the epistle, from chapter 1:18 all the way up to 3:23, and again in 8:1 when he says, "We know that we all have knowledge. Knowledge puffs up, but love edifies." Likewise, the problem of gifts and their use occupies much of his thought, especially in chapters 12–14. These two issues provide the majority of the material for Paul's discussion throughout the letter. The Corinthians were convinced of the supremacy of their knowledge and of their gifts.

In this way, with much that was good, they embodied all that could be bad in a church. As we shall see in the next chapter, 1 Corinthians 13 comes right in the middle of this, addressing questions such as, "What is the remedy to pride?" It is central to the development of thought in the book, and directly relevant to Paul's concern for the Corinthian church.

The Problem of Gifts

Chapters 12–14 address the problems of the use of gifts in this Christian assembly. In chapter 12, the unity and diversity of the church comes to the fore. The church is one body, consisting of many parts, with much diversity among the members. Notice, for example, verses 4–6: "There are diversities of gifts, but the same Spirit. There are differences of ministries, but the same Lord. And there are diversities of activities, but it is the same God who works all in all." There is a great variety, yet none have all that was good or necessary or edifying. Even the apostles must recognize the diversity in the church, "God has appointed these in the church: first apostles, second prophets, third teachers, after that miracles, then gifts of healings, helps, administrations, varieties of tongues. Are all apostles? Are all prophets? Are all teachers? Are all workers of miracles?" (12:28–29).

In chapter 14, the apostle moves from the general problem of gifts to the specific area of tongues and prophecy. Apparently, there were many who believed that their gift of tongues was superior to everything else, and they used it as a proud display. Notice several verses, "Since you are zealous for spiritual gifts, let it be for the edification of the church that you seek to excel"; "For God is not the author of confusion but of peace, as in all the churches of the saints"; "Let all things be done decently and in order" (14:12, 33, 40). The use of gifts, intended to edify, was instead creating a tremendous problem in the church.

In the midst of these two chapters, we find our chapter about love. It comes between them as a vital digression. While the Corinthians had fallen in love with their gifts, pressing these to a prideful extreme, they must be brought back to reality. Love, true love, is the only context in which these gifts are to be expressed. The goal is not the gift, but the grace, and the grace of love must have priority over the gift.

The Way Beyond Comparison

Does Paul set love against gifts, or wisdom, or knowledge? Not at all. These things are vital for the church. But if they are to be used with profit, and not just for personal profit but for the good of the whole church, they must be set in the context of love. What is the motive of all Christian activity? There is only one answer—it is love. Gifts are good to use, as is knowledge, but the best way for them to be used is in love.

Corinth, with all of its benefits and blessings in the church—wisdom and knowledge and unsurpassed gifts—was a church with much failure, because pride took the place of love. Their church life had become like an orchestra playing different pieces of music at the same time: one playing Beethoven, another Mozart, another Shostakovich and another Copeland. All of them may be talented musicians, but as they battle each other, the beauty of the music is lost in the din of sound.

How was the Corinthian church to function? By love. Paul does not seek to diminish their knowledge, nor does he even seek to curtail the varied expressions of gifts. He simply seeks to restore the heart and soul to their church life, in a God-centred exercise of love.

Corinth in the 21st Century

It is really easy to look back at the Corinthians and their problems with a detached sense of sorrow, thinking to ourselves, "Isn't it sad that a church so blessed could stumble so badly?" While it is right to have this kind of concern, it comes far short of the proper response we ought to have. For most of us in the West, we fail to recognize ourselves in these descriptions of the Corinthians—and yet we are right there.

While we may not be so crass as to say these things, we often think of them: *We are the heirs of the Reformation. We have more teachers, more books, more scholars, and more resources than ever. The fruit of twenty centuries of Christian study fills our bookshelves, our devices, and our favourite websites. We give more to missions, we send more workers to the harvest field, than any other time in history, and our churches are strong and healthy. We are conquering the world for Christ!*

And yet is it possible that we are more like the Corinthians than we like to admit? Are we proud of the blessings which come only from God? Do we boast in our knowledge, in our "spiritual" wealth, in our positions of leadership? We smugly credit ourselves with the advance of Christianity in the modern age, as if it is due to our influence. Have we forgotten that *everything* we have comes from the Lord, and thus we have no right to take pride in it? These problems are at the very root of our weakness and lethargy, and often we are completely unaware! We pride ourselves in what has been done, and in who we are, forgetting that nothing is accomplished apart from the Lord and his powerful work. Are you pleased with your Christianity? Do you compare your church with others, thinking that it is better, bigger, purer? If so, you are a Corinthian. And you desperately need Paul's message, as do I.

As we work our way through 1 Corinthians 13, we must constantly bring ourselves back to these issues. Every church must, in the ongoing activity of its ministries, return to this root. It is possible to have much wisdom and knowledge; to be full of gifts; and yet lose sight of the great need for true and unfeigned love. Knowledge puffs up, gifts provide cause for boasting, even charitable deeds become a source of pride. And love is pushed out of the door.

Should knowledge cease? Are gifts unnecessary and irrelevant? Is benevolence wasted energy? No, never. But without love, they are only a broken shell of what they should be. Will you give careful attention to this passage, asking yourself if you are like the Corinthians, with much that is good and commendable, and yet lacking in love?

May God help us to learn from his holy Word.

Chapter 3
WITHOUT LOVE; OR 5–1=0

Though I speak with the tongues of men and of angels, but have not love, I have become sounding brass or a clanging cymbal. And though I have the gift of prophecy, and understand all mysteries and all knowledge, and though I have all faith, so that I could remove mountains, but have not love, I am nothing. And though I bestow all my goods to feed the poor, and though I give my body to be burned, but have not love, it profits me nothing.
1 Corinthians 13:1–3

Sometimes, God's arithmetic is different from our own. I do not mean that when God adds 2+2 he comes up with something other than 4, but rather that his perspective on life and its relationships far surpasses our own. One commentator, after he has completed his exposition of verses 1–3, summarized their teaching with this simple equation: 5–1=0.[5]

Paul here mentions five activities.

[5] D. A. Carson, *Showing the Spirit: A Theological Exposition of 1 Corinthians 12–14* (Grand Rapids: Baker, 1987), 60.

1. Speaking with the tongues of men and of angels;
2. Having the gift of prophecy and understanding all mysteries and all knowledge;
3. Having all faith to remove mountains;
4. Bestowing goods to feed the poor;
5. Giving his body to be burned.

All of these were important to or present in the life of the Corinthian church, and all empty without the grace of love.

Paul addresses a very real problem existing among the believers at Corinth. In the midst of the wonderful things God has done with them, self-importance crept into their lives. They have slipped into a mode of thinking in which they congratulated themselves for their spiritual attainments, as if they were responsible for these things. Now, puffed up with arrogance, they must consider their actions and gifts and experiences.

There is a subtle, but very important change from 1 Corinthians 12 to chapter 13. As he writes of love, Paul personalizes his description with the pronoun "I". This is a fascinating method of communication. It is not simply pointing the finger at them, as he does at other times in the epistle (notice chapters 5 and 6). It is rather a wonderful means of seeking to engage their hearts by way of their minds. They must think through these things, since they apply not just generally, but even to the great apostle himself. Paul's use of "I" makes this chapter very personal—and this is his intent. As he pens these words, his concern is that each one listening or reading would incorporate themselves into his descriptions, and examine their own hearts. Remember, 5–1=0. Without love, even the best of actions are worthless.

What is love?

We will look in vain to find a clear-cut definition of love in these verses. Paul's purpose is not fine-tuned analysis and technical precision. Rather, he is concerned with description.. Paul approaches love in the way that we might seek to speak of a flower. What is a flower? Few, if any, of us would respond with a scientific definition. Instead, we would attempt to use our powers of description. One might tell of a beautiful blossom, radiant in colour and fragrance, while another might describe the stem and the bud glistening in the morning dew. Each description would reflect the individual's thought. In the same way that a tulip differs from a rose and both differ from an orchid, so the descriptions would differ, yet all would be true. Paul, in 1 Corinthians 13, is not exhaustive in his representation of love. Rather, he is suggestive. As a wise pastor, with the peculiar needs of the Christians at Corinth in mind, he presents love in the facets best suited to their needs. There is much in the rest of Scripture to fill out a definition of love.

There is a matter that needs to be cleared up at this point. A popular notion, commonly spread in pulpits and Bible studies, misrepresents the words for love used in the Greek of the New Testament. It is said that the word *agapē* is a special word for God's love—a kind of sacrificial divine love—while *philia* is a less powerful word, used for friendship and little more. This idea needs to be closely examined. Not very far from our context, in 1 Corinthians 16: 22 and 24, we find Paul using these two Greek words in close proximity. Examining them in English, one cannot discern any difference in meaning between them. In verse 22, the lack of love for the Lord Jesus Christ brings a curse, while in verse 24 the author expresses his love for all of them. In both cases, love is a deep, whole-souled attachment. One uses *agapē* and the other uses *philia*. But what is surprising is that verse 22 uses a form of *philia*, and verse 24 uses *agapē*. This is not what one might expect if the above notion were correct.

Similarly, there is a phrase used in John 3:35 and 5:20 that is identical in our English translation: "The father loves the Son." But John uses forms of *agapē* in the first and *philia* in the second. Who can discern the difference between the two? Perhaps even more revealingly, when Demas is described as having forsaken Paul in 2 Timothy 4:10, it is said that the reason is that he "loved this present world". The word for love is a form of *agapē*. In 2 Samuel 13:1, 4, 15, the Septuagint, the Greek translation of the Hebrew Old Testament, uses the same term *agapē* to describe Amnon's lust for his half-sister Tamar.

While *agapē* is often used to express God's love, it does not inherently carry the sense of sacrificial divine love. In some ways, it is similar in meaning to *philia*. Scholars tell us that in about 400 BC, *agapē* began to grow in prominence in the Greek language. *Philia*, among other things, was associated with kissing, while *agapē* was not. They are not perfect synonyms, but there is significant overlap.

So, what is love? We might say that it is a combination of affection and action, or perhaps better, it is action suffused with affection. It is a holy attachment of one person to another (or to the truth, or the church) in which both heart and hand express the reality. It is the inward sense of longing, desire and delight, and it is the outward expression of appropriate words and deeds. It is the combination of inner and outer behaviour which focuses on someone else. For example, the Scripture plainly states, "God is love." As the perfect illustration, God shows us what love is. In Isaiah 62:4, he tells his people that he delights in them, a frequent and recurrent theme in the Bible. In Romans 5:8, we read that he proves, or demonstrates, his love by sending his Son to die for sinners. Love is inward and outward; affection and action; emotion and motion. This is what Paul speaks of in 1 Corinthians 13.

What is love's importance?

At the very beginning of this chapter, Paul is concerned to demonstrate the importance of love. The Corinthian Christians needed to know that love was at the very centre of a genuinely God-honouring life.

It is possible to do great things without love. In this case, it seems certain that this was at the root of the Corinthian problem. But we should notice a principle clearly taught in these verses: outward action, without inward reality, is nothing. For these believers, the problem was not a passive monastic retreat from the world, but rather a confidence in religious activism, yet without heart—outward deeds, minus the engagement of genuine emotion. Using himself as the object of attention ("I"), Paul speaks through contrasts.[6] Each articulates an activity, or cluster of activities, in themselves very good and positive—the first three being divine acts, and the last two, noble acts of human benevolence and fidelity.

The first mentions the practice of *speaking in tongues* in the Corinthian church.[7] Clearly, they were experts at this Spirit-given practice, as chapter 14 makes abundantly clear. It seems that every one of their meetings was blessed with manifestations of this divine gift. Probably, for the Corinthians, speaking in tongues was viewed as the supreme spiritual ability, marking out the mature believer. Paul's use of this practice as his first illustration would certainly capture their attention.

The second turns the reader's attention to related supernatural

---

[6] In the Greek text, the structure of these verses is somewhat clearer than in English. Paul writes a sequence of five clauses, all of them separated by the words kai ean or kan (which is a contraction of kai ean). These words mark out the divisions in thought expressed by the apostle and serve as the division markers for our exposition. In the New King James Version, the appearances of the word "though" mark out the divisions.

[7] This is not the place to discuss the use of tongues today. I would recommend that the reader consult O. Palmer Robertson's *The Final Word* (Edinburgh: Banner of Truth, 1993) for a helpful discussion of that issue.

activities: *prophecy*, and the understanding of all mysteries and knowledge. Prophecy may be either fore-telling (future prediction) or forth-telling (preaching). All mysteries are the things that God himself has hidden from some only to reveal to others, while knowledge may be the possession of all "the observable, knowable facts of the created universe, being virtually omniscient".[8] Paul is picking up some of the threads of the discussion presented in 12:8–10. He is not describing natural endowments—abilities common to human beings. He is rather speaking of divinely granted capacities, once again directly related to the charismatic experiences of the Corinthian Christians.

The third, *having all faith to remove mountains*, carries on the theme of supernatural activity in accomplishment. Faith here is not saving faith related to justification, common to all believers, but is a special gift of faith to act on God's promises. The language used reminds the reader of the words of Jesus in Matthew 17:20: "if you have faith as a mustard seed, you will say to this mountain, 'Move from here to there,' and it will move; and nothing will be impossible for you." This would be a tremendous ability, once again directly relevant to the Corinthian fascination with spectacular supernatural acts.

The fourth item in Paul's series turns away from the practice of the supernatural and describes a different kind of facet of genuine godliness—*benevolence*. He speaks in terms of supreme generosity, giving all of his goods for the sake of the poor. One wonders whether the apostle had another saying of Jesus in mind: "One thing you lack: Go your way, sell whatever you have and give to the poor, and you will have treasure in heaven; and come, take up the cross, and follow Me" (Mark 10:21). It is said that the rabbis taught that the maximum gift

---

[8] John MacArthur, *1 Corinthians: MacArthur New Testament Commentary*, (Chicago: Moody Press, 1984), 333.

necessary to demonstrate charity was twenty per cent of one's goods.[9] Paul says that he might give it all—an enormous sacrifice.

The last in the series may well be the most dramatic. The final offering that anyone may make is *martyrdom*, and Paul envisions such for himself here.[10] Burning at the stake must be one of the most excruciating deaths imaginable, an opportunity to demonstrate utter loyalty to a cause. It would only be about ten years before some Christians would be called on to make this very sacrifice under the wicked reign of Nero. Isn't this the greatest and noblest of Christian acts?

Paul says that all of these surpassingly great works of God and men—supernatural acts of revelation and personal sacrifice without equal—are nothing without love. They are utterly empty and devoid of any significance or power. They might as well never have been performed, because they flow from a faulty base. Without love, these amazing things are nothing.

Without love, speaking in tongues becomes like a sounding brass and a clanging cymbal, annoying sounds without any redeeming value. Have you ever listened to a percussionist practising without the orchestra? The repetition of sounds without melody or harmony grates on the ear and the consciousness. It has been pointed out that in New Testament times, some pagan worship services included ecstatic utterances accompanied by smashing gongs, clanging cymbals, and blaring trumpets.[11] If this were the case, these Corinthians should have quickly understood his point. Without love, their exercise of gifts is worth no more than it would be among pagans. Or perhaps to sharpen the point even more, it is possible that their worship services,

---

[9] Ibid., 335.

[10] There is a textual variant present in the text. Some manuscripts read "to be burned", while others read "that I may boast". In either case, the body is being offered up sacrificially.

[11] MacArthur, *1 Corinthians*, 331.

characterized on the one hand with the spectacular gifts, and on the other hand by division and pride, were no better than the empty rituals of the pagans. Harsh criticism indeed!

In 13:2, prophecy, mysteries, knowledge, and faith to remove mountains, receive similar treatment, though Paul's point is more personal. He says that if he has the ability to know and do all these things, but has not love, he is still nothing. The emphasis is on the personal experience of doing God's works and knowing God's thoughts—prophecy, mysteries, knowledge; and even having the faith described by Jesus to move mountains. But without love, they are absolutely worthless. Paul's Greek is very plain and simple. Possession of the charismata—the supernatural gifts—is not the sign of spiritual life. Christian love is. Knowledge and wisdom in all their forms, however expressed, are nothing—worthless, useless, empty, zero.

The contrast in 13:3 turns to the personal sacrifices Paul might make: giving away all of his goods to the poor and offering his body to be sacrificed. These are the extremes of benevolence and dedication, the most astounding acts that a human might make. But without love, they too are nothing. They are only self-serving deeds intended to puff up the individual, and the only "benefit" is a sinful sense of self-accomplishment. Apparently, not only is it possible to gain the whole world and lose the soul, but it is also possible to give the whole world and lose the soul. We must remember Jesus' words about those who "do [their] charitable deeds before men" (see Matt. 6:1–4). Their rewards are only found in the empty accolades of men. These great acts bring *nothing* of value to one's life, if unaccompanied by love. Even as an apostle, without love at the centre of his emotion and action, Paul is nothing. 5–1=0.

The Bottom Line

The personalization of these truths was intended to make the Corinthians think of the application to their own lives. In the same way, we too ought to personalize this teaching. One commentator, writing on this passage, illustrates this:

> The easiest way to move this paragraph from their situation to ours is simply to give it a new … expression, in terms of how one thinks of his/her own life to be spiritually significant. For example, "If I preach with the brilliance of Paul or Chrysostom, but have not love…"; or perhaps, "If I write a commentary on 1 Corinthians 13, but have not love…"[12]

We could easily expand this idea: "Though I—home school my children and carefully order my family; serve as an officer or Sunday school teacher in my church, or as a professor in a theological seminary; read only the best of Christian books; pay my taxes and settle all my debts; visit the sick and elderly, give generously to my church; raise my children to be foreign missionaries—but have not love, I am nothing." This is a startling perspective on our Christian lives. It challenges our values and our self-perceptions. Are the things that seem so very important to us, at the very heart of our Christian identities, truly motivated by this grace? Or do we do them for other reasons?

Another author has written:

> If Paul were addressing the modern church, perhaps he would (press the application) further: You Christians, who prove your

---

[12] Gordon Fee, *The First Epistle to the Corinthians: The New International Commentary on the New Testament* (Grand Rapids: Eerdmans, 1987), 635.

> spirituality by the amount of theological information you can cram into your heads, I tell you that such knowledge by itself proves nothing. And you who affirm the Spirit's presence in your meetings because there is a certain style of worship (whether formal and stately or exuberant and spontaneous), if your worship patterns are not expressions of love, you are spiritually bankrupt.[13]

We all need to examine our hearts. In what areas of the Christian life do you think that you excel? In what aspect of Christian service are you involved? Whatever you do, if it is without love, it is nothing. The Corinthians were guilty of putting a feather in their caps every time they did something for God, and then assuming that they were important. This is like a man who drives a long distance and then brags about all of the bridges he passed. Do these make him important? Neither do their actions. Without love, they are null and void—totally useless. Yet they were puffed up over them. What a strange twisting of reality. But we all do the same things frequently.

There is another application crying out for our attention. I must make it with reference to my own doctrinal tradition, but it may apply to many other theological and denominational groupings as well. If the diagnosis is true of your church tradition, please take the remedy. Evangelicals as a whole, and often those who hold to the Reformed Faith in particular, may be prone to a besetting sin contrary to is the love written about in these verses. Because we live in a world so opposed to the gospel, and in a Christian culture that is often confused by error and disagreement, we quickly and easily fall prey to our knowledge. The Reformed Faith has always been known for its careful study of Scripture, its well-developed statements of theology

[13] Carson, *Showing the Spirit*, 61.

expressed in confessions of faith, its excellent perception of the fulness of Christian teaching. Unhappily, it has also often been marked by a cold orthodoxy and a triumphant spirit, superior to those who differ. This is knowledge without love, forgetting the words written earlier in 1 Corinthians, "Knowledge puffs up, but love edifies" (8:1). Our well-developed statements of doctrine and practice are not handled with compassion and patience, but with pride of knowledge and force of expression. May God forgive us! We must guard against this danger in our own hearts; too often, I have sinned in this very area—glad to know the details of the truth and ready to denigrate others who differ. Do you have love? How do you relate to someone from another church who differs with you over your particular doctrinal distinctives? Or, who has a different view of eschatology, or many other things? We must not do away with knowledge, but rather, learn to express it by love. We must be "swift to hear" and "slow to speak" (Jas. 1:19), willing to treat our brothers and sisters with grace because of the grace of the God we serve and proclaim.

I would urge you to examine your heart in general and be aware of this danger in particular, seeking to show to the world the love without which we are nothing. 5–1=0. May God help us to pursue love.

Chapter 4
THE ACTS OF LOVE

Love suffers long and is kind...
1 Corinthians 13:4

Christian love is emotion in action; not just one or the other. In the first three verses of this chapter many activities are presented, all commendable, including supreme acts of benevolence, all of them are worthless without love. From this we learn that we must not define this Christian grace only in terms of deeds. In 1 Corinthians 13:4–7, however, Paul turns around, and in describing the qualities of love, instead emphasizes actions.

Paul's words are captivating and full of life, though they may be somewhat unexpected. Normally, when we describe something, we do so by means of adjectives and nouns. We might say something such as "Happiness is sunshine in the soul after the clouds of trouble; cool refreshing water for the thirst of the weary traveller." We rely on phrases full of nouns and adjectives to present a picture. Paul does not do this. His description of love mainly uses verbs—action words—as if love were a living thing, able to think and move and do. Love, pictured here, is the action of our hearts: it gives and receives; it acts and refrains from acting. It is not merely a philosophical concept, rich and beautiful in expression, but it is the fulness of sanctified behaviour, actively responding to what is around. For all of this, we must notice that none of these things are emotional or sentimental. They all have to do with our deeds.

Paul uses a very interesting structure in expressing himself. From verse 4 to verse 7, the apostle uses fifteen verbs to describe love. He begins with two positive statements, then eight negatives, followed by five further positives. The final negative is coupled with its positive opposite, and the last four positives become nearly universal in reference. The final quality—endurance—is very similar to the first and leads to one more statement at the beginning of verse 8, seeking to describe love's permanence. We shall seek to study each of these qualities—these actions—of love. Let us turn to the first pair: love suffers long and is kind. Each of these is an aspect of love's response to the actions of others.

Love Suffers Long

Our English translation renders Paul's first words as "Love suffers long." This is a good translation, both in terms of definition and form, carrying over to our language the sense of the action of love. The Greek word behind this rendering is rich and full of meaning. It speaks of relationships between people and goes immediately to the heart of problems that often enter such relationships. Paul is not slow to get to the very centre of love's acts. The word means "forbearance", the ability to be inconvenienced or taken advantage of by a person over and over again, without becoming angry in response. The early Christian preacher John Chrysostom said, "It is a word which is used of the man who is wronged and who has it easily in his power to avenge himself, but who will never do it."[14] Patience *never* retaliates.

To suffer long is the opposite of being short-tempered. Sometimes we speak of angry people who quickly fall prey to this side

[14] Quoted in MacArthur, *1 Corinthians*, 338.

of their emotions, describing them as "hot-heads" or "short-fused". They exhibit the converse of the gracious act Paul seeks to describe. Love that suffers long is willing to receive blows, whether physical, emotional, or social, and not pay back in kind, in reality, in any way at all. Love that *suffers long* looks beyond the temptation to strike back with word or fist or by any other means. It loves the one who has done the wrong, and thus cannot and will not meet sin with sin. It must stay separate from the tit-for-tat mentality of personal relationships, for it says, "Though you did such to me, and perhaps will do more of the same, I will continue to receive it, for I love you. I will not injure you, though you injure me."

John MacArthur points out that suffering long is a peculiarly Christian virtue. He writes:

> In the Greek world, self-sacrificing love and non-avenging patience were considered weaknesses, unworthy of the noble man or woman. Aristotle, for example, taught that the great Greek virtue was refusal to tolerate insult or injury and to strike back in retaliation for the slightest offence. Vengeance was a virtue.[15]

This sounds a lot like the get-even philosophy of our own culture: "If you step on my toes, I will step on yours"; and by doing so, we dominate over others. But love suffers long. This is Christian love, appropriate for this letter. Paul wants the Corinthians to understand that this is the way that they must act. In 1 Corinthians 6, the apostle confronted their sinful willingness to take brothers to court, before the judges of the world. In 6:7, he called this an utter failure. It would have been better, more loving, to suffer wrong than to insist on their own

[15] Ibid., 338.

rights. One is reminded of Proverbs 19:11: "The discretion of a man makes him slow to anger, and his glory is to overlook a transgression."

The Scriptures provide us with several helpful illustrations. Do you remember the story that our Lord Jesus told, recorded in Matthew 18:23–27, about the man who owed a great debt to his master? We are told that his indebtedness was so staggering that only by selling the servant, along with his wife and children, could payment be made. When the servant heard of this plan, he fell down before his lord, asking for patience (the same word that Paul uses), promising to repay everything that he owed. The master was moved with compassion, released the servant from custody, and forgave the debt. Jesus told this story in response to a question from his disciples: "Lord, how often shall my brother sin against me, and I forgive him? Up to seven times?" (Matt. 18:21). Just as the master is God-like in his willingness to forgive, and so also must all of Jesus' disciples be. It is of real interest to note that as the story continues, the forgiven servant fails to extend the same grace to his debtors that he had received from his lord. This brings upon him even greater punishment than previously had been promised—his master delivers him to torture. Jesus' final words are a warning to all: "So My heavenly Father also will do to you if each of you, from his heart, does not forgive his brother his trespasses." Love suffers long.

Similarly, Peter tells us that God himself abundantly exhibits this holy grace towards his enemies, sinners, when he says in 2 Peter 3:9: "The Lord is not slack concerning His promise, as some count slackness, but is longsuffering toward us, not willing that any should perish but that all should come to repentance." While some misunderstand God's apparent reluctance to send judgement upon sinners, thinking that it means he is uninterested, this very reluctance is an expression of his mercy. He withholds wrath, calling men to repent. How often in the

Old Testament do we read of the Lord's holding back his wrath from his people when they sinned? Do you remember Jesus' lament over Jerusalem? It was his last public pronouncement, and is very moving: "O Jerusalem, Jerusalem, the one who kills the prophets and stones those who are sent to her! How often I wanted to gather your children together, as a hen gathers her chicks under her wings, but you were not willing!" (Matt. 23:37).

Eminently, our Lord Jesus exemplifies the patience described here. All of his earthly life was a period of humiliation, endured for us, and yet he never complained. Though Calvary cast its shadow across every step of his path, he persevered to the end. With prophetic insight, Isaiah says of him, "He was oppressed and He was afflicted, yet He opened not His mouth; He was led as a lamb to the slaughter, and as a sheep before its shearers is silent, so He opened not His mouth" (Isa. 53:7). Peter, meditating on the words of the prophet, said this:

> ...Christ also suffered for us, leaving us an example, that you should follow His steps:
>
> "Who committed no sin,
> Nor was deceit found in His mouth";
>
> who, when He was reviled, did not revile in return; when He suffered, He did not threaten, but committed Himself to Him who judges righteously; who Himself bore our sins in His own body on the tree, that we, having died to sins, might live for righteousness—by whose stripes you were healed. For you were like sheep going astray, but have now returned to the Shepherd and Overseer of your souls. (1 Pet. 2:21–25)

Love suffers long. It bears with offences, refuses to retaliate. During the last week or month, did you face a situation like one of these? Did someone take advantage of you or harm you in word or deed? What did you do? If you are like most of us, you may have responded with similar words or actions. We frequently strike back when we are hurt. But as Christians, as disciples of Jesus, we must seek to do far better. Your Saviour endured, and he knows how to help everyone facing similar temptations. Rely on him for strength, and by his grace show how true love acts when it is provoked. Do you remember what we learned in chapter 1 of this book—we love him because he first loved us? Here it is again. As Peter said, Christ's patient self-sacrifice ought to produce righteousness in us! Look to Christ and be strong in the things of God. Remember that love suffers long.

Love is Kind

The companion to the longsuffering of love is kindness. While the first speaks of the absence of retaliation, the second presents the positive response love gives when dealing with others. In the Greek, this is the only place in the New Testament where this verb is found; but the noun helps us to understand the meaning of our word. Among its senses are such ideas as "useful, suitable, worthy, good; pleasant, kindly, benevolent". One author has said that it means "quick to pay back with kindness what it received in hurt".[16] We should think of it as the expression of love and mercy poured out on an offender, despite his offence. It is more than a demeanour of benevolence; it is the payment of good for evil. Proverbs 25:21–22 says, "If your enemy is hungry, give him bread to eat; and if he is thirsty, give him water to drink; for so you will heap coals of fire on his head, and the LORD will reward you."

[16] Carson, *Showing the Spirit*, 62.

In some ways, our English translation cannot do justice to this word. Paul is not simply saying that love is kind, describing an attribute of love; he says that love acts kindly, even toward its enemies. Perhaps we should say "love kindnesses". This is not proper English, but it makes the point. "Love is kind" implies a passive attribute of love; "love kindnesses" presents the activity of love. To a variety of circumstances, even provocation of the most grievous kind, love replies with grace and mercy. Scholars tell us that, not only is this verb found just once in the New Testament, it is also only found in Christian writings. Did Paul coin the term because this aspect of love is unique to Christianity?

We may notice many illustrations of this active love in the Scriptures, but two will suffice here. In his Sermon on the Mount, Jesus said:

> "You have heard that it was said, 'An eye for an eye and a tooth for a tooth.' But I tell you not to resist an evil person. But whoever slaps you on your right cheek, turn the other to him also. If anyone wants to sue you and take away your tunic, let him have your cloak also. And whoever compels you to go one mile, go with him two. Give to him who asks you, and from him who wants to borrow from you do not turn away. (Matt. 5:38–42)

Our Saviour's words directly address the issue at hand. Love does not evaluate the worthiness of its object, and then act, as if saying, "I will be kind to this one, but not that one"; it must extend even to enemies: a legal opponent, even a Roman soldier. Can you imagine how strange such ideas would have been to his hearers? In one example, the Romans, with the power compel people to go miles, were the oppressors, emissaries of a foreign power, soldiers of a despised tyrannical enemy. Or, in the other example, is a lawsuit ever carried out in a climate of kindness or courtesy? Is it not, almost by definition, a place of animosity between adversaries? And yet these two circumstances make the point. Love "kindnesses"—it is different from the world. It willingly gives, even to those who are seeking to harm. It reaches out to its enemies with a cup of water and a loaf of bread. It crucifies the desire for retaliation and calls out for blessing instead.

Perhaps even more basic is Paul's comment in Romans 11:22: "Therefore consider the goodness and severity of God: on those who fell, severity; but toward you, goodness, if you continue in His goodness. Otherwise, you also will be cut off." In this case, goodness is a translation of a word directly related to kindness. Notice that the apostle begins with the word "therefore". Earlier in the context of this chapter (and really, in the whole epistle), he had discussed the considerable provocation offered to God by both Jews and Gentiles. In the midst of this, God demonstrated his eternal kindness, even to his enemies, in the sending of his Son (Rom. 5:8). But even greater than this, not merely sending the Son but sending him to die in the place of sinners—to bear divine wrath to the uttermost. If ever there was a true commendation of divine goodness, here it is. God is kind to his enemies.

Kindness is Christ crying out to his Father, "Forgive them, for they do not know what they do" (Luke 23:34), even after all that he had faced from these same men. They had mocked him, spat upon him, plucked out his beard, turned his back into ribbons of red-hot flesh and blood, yet he still looked upon them with compassion.

In Romans 2:4, Paul brings together these two qualities of love, "Or do you despise the riches of His goodness, forbearance, and longsuffering, not knowing that the goodness of God leads you to repentance?" Kindness (the word goodness here) and longsuffering are the nature of God. When in 1 Corinthians 13:4 Paul places the same ideas together, he draws upon the nature of God's love. Love suffers long, and "kindnesses", since God's love suffers long—it is full of patience, and responds to its enemies, even the wicked provocations of sinners, by reaching out through the beloved Son.

Examining Our Love

None of us will be able to say that our love matches these two positive declarations about Christian love. All of us face situations that test the nature of our love. What do you do when someone offends you? When they decide, without just cause, to be your enemy? When they don't like you and seek to injure or harass you? The most natural response, in every one of our hearts, is to take offence and strike back. But what does the gospel say? Our love for others must prevent us from doing this. We desperately need the help of God's Holy Spirit to change us. By his grace, our love can grow and blossom into a fragrant gospel fruit—the fruit of the Spirit—which is love.

Do you suffer long? Are you able to receive the insults and indignities of life without taking offence? We live in a fallen world, and offences must come. When they come, how do you respond? Is there anyone against whom you hold a grudge today? It could be your spouse, or your parents or children; perhaps your employer or co-workers, your neighbour, or even fellow Christians. If you do this, you do not truly love that person. Search your heart, and by the grace of God seek repentance and renewal.

Is your love kind? Do you seek to show kindness, even to those who despitefully use you? Do you have anyone, who has taken offence against you, to whom you can show kindness? If you are not willing, you don't have love.

We may return to the first three verses of our chapter: love must be action; it takes priority over gifts and knowledge and sacrifices. Do you love?

The following story helps to make our point:

> One of Abraham Lincoln's earliest political enemies was Edwin M. Stanton. He called Lincoln a "low cunning gorilla" and "the original gorilla". "It was ridiculous for people to go to Africa to see a gorilla," he would say, "when they could find one easily in Springfield, Illinois." Lincoln never responded to the slander, but when, as president, he needed a secretary of war, he chose Stanton. When his incredulous friends asked why, Lincoln replied, "Because he is the best man." Years later, as the slain president's body lay in state, Stanton looked into the coffin and said through his tears, "There lies the greatest ruler of men the world has ever seen." His animosity was finally broken by Lincoln's long-suffering, non-retaliatory spirit. Patient love won out.[17]

This is what we must be. Will you seek to love like this? May God help us to bear patiently in love.

---

[17] MacArthur, *1 Corinthians,* 339.

Chapter 5
LOVE AND SELF

love does not envy;
love does not parade itself, is not puffed up…
1 Corinthians 13:4

"Love does not…" As we proceed further into our exposition of Paul's words, we find a long string of negatives—eight in all. The apostle wants us to consider several aspects of human behaviour, each one common to us all, and every one antithetical to love.

Most of us would consider ourselves to be loving people. We each evaluate our lives, and conclude that, to some degree or another, we love. The words before us, however, ought to make us look again. Who among us—who in all the world—exhibits the long-suffering and kindness described at the beginning of verse 4? As we have considered, we must admit that we seldom are able to tolerate offences, never mind show the type of long-suffering placed before us here. We fall far short of true love.

Here we learn more about our subject. Paul's use of negative words is striking. He is a good teacher, understanding how best to impart his lessons to his pupils. It would have been possible to use positive words; for example, the apostle might have said, "Love is contented; love is humble." But he chose to use words that bring conviction to our minds. The Spirit of God, the ultimate Author of these words, moved Paul to write as he did for our benefit. He seeks to search our hearts with the deep things of God, speaking to us through the Scriptures not merely to increase our knowledge, but to change our behaviour. Will you listen as he deals with you?

Love Does Not Envy

The first negative aspect of love—emotion in action—is that it does not envy. In the original language, an interesting word is used. Our English word zeal is derived from the Greek word we find here. It means envy or jealousy, and may have a good or a bad connotation. The context is the determining factor.

In 1 Corinthians 14, for example, the word is used twice in its good sense. Paul says, "desire spiritual gifts" in verse 1, and "desire earnestly to prophesy" in verse 39. In both cases, he urges them to have zeal for good things. Similarly, in Galatians 4:18 he says, "It is good to be zealous in a good thing always…" Here, Paul contrasts his ministry and teaching with that of the Judaizers—a group whose teachings confused law and gospel and were deeply troubling the churches of Galatia. While they were "zealous" in their proselytising efforts (4:17), seeking to persuade the Galatian Christians of their heretical brand of doctrine, Paul urges these believers to be zealous for the truth. They must desire it, seek it with jealousy. For a good cause, the word can describe a praiseworthy longing.

But more often we think of envy as a bad thing. Examples are not difficult to produce. In Acts 7:9, we read that Stephen, standing before the Jewish Council, reminds these men of one of the sad events in the history of Israel—"the patriarchs, becoming envious, sold Joseph into Egypt." The sons of Jacob, brothers and heirs of the promises given by God to their father, were jealous of the affection and attention showered by their elderly father on his young son. They could not accept the fact that though he was young—the eleventh of twelve sons—he was destined to be the most prominent of them. He dreamed that they would bow down to him; he received the "many-coloured" coat from Jacob, and they envied him. Their emotions were so great that they conspired together to injure him and ultimately sold him into slavery, reporting to their father that he had been killed by a wild beast. They did not care about the heartbreak Jacob would endure. The ugly passion of their envy brought great suffering to their brother and their aging father. It was a terrible sin; and this is exactly what Paul means in using this word in our text.

Love does not envy; it does not behave like Joseph's brothers. It does not allow the prosperity of another to become a source of contention or a desire to do harm. This quality of love has a direct application to the Corinthians: it clearly refers to the divisions that had erupted in their midst. Paul told them, in 1 Corinthians 3:3, that envy was one of the sinful passions causing the carnal bickering present in their church. It was jealousy that caused the strife and party spirit among them. Even in the Christian assembly, one looked at another and envied—perhaps gifts and abilities, or prominence in the church, even perhaps friendships with well-known Christian leaders (Paul, Apollos, Cephas, Christ—see 1:12). The private thoughts of envy burst forth into words and actions. At first, envy was just a thought: "I wish that I could have what you have; I wish I had your gifts; I wish I had your friends." But it did not stop there and began to section off the church. One segment rivalled another segment, and the godly unity of the church was divided—all with the appearance of spirituality, but driven by envy. Once jealousy begins, it is exceedingly difficult to reign in. A flame under a pot of water will eventually cause the contents to boil over, unable to be contained, and bringing pain to anyone who touches it. Envy is just the same. Left unchecked, it will rise up and cause great grief and injury.

Envy is the opposite of contentment. Well-instructed Christians understand that God in his wise providence gives to some and withholds from others, according to his own holy will. When they seem to have less than others, they know that it is the Lord's disposition to them, and they bow in reverent acceptance. Jealousy is not like this. It dethrones God, viewing self as the deserving centre of blessing. Contentment rests in a holy trust, able to rejoice at the things God has done for others. Jealousy boils at the benefits enjoyed by another. The apostle makes this point clearly in 3:5–9. Using himself and Apollos as examples, he poses the question, "What are we but servants sent by the Lord?" Whatever they do, and whatever the results, they are utterly dependent on the acts of God. If he chooses to bless their work, they give him glory. If he chooses to withhold his power, they bow in adoration. In either case, it is the Lord who acts. We simply watch and worship. The worker is nothing, because it is God at work in all. Love *cannot* envy, gladly rejoicing in whatever God does, wherever and whenever he does it.

As Paul writes to the Corinthians, and to us, he asserts that love does not envy—a rare quality indeed. But he would have his readers pause and consider themselves. How do you respond to the good things that happen to others? When your co-worker receives a larger pay increase than you do? When someone else is asked to do something you believe you could do better? When recognition goes to someone else? There are few who have mastered the grace of being content, without envy, simply because they love. It all comes back to your view of God. Do you really believe that he is in control?

These questions lead us to our next phrase.

Love Does Not Parade Itself

Not only must envy be absent from true love, but so also must be pride and arrogance. Just as love's contentment trusts in divine sovereignty, so love's humility bows before divine majesty.

We read that "Love does not parade itself" (13:4). At this point, our author does something very interesting. Again, Paul uses a word that is found nowhere else in the Bible; in fact, this is the earliest known occurrence of the word in any literature. He seems to introduce, or possibly coin, a word to make his point. Our translation of the word is visually striking, making us think of men walking in a parade, with banners and life-size portraits carried by supporters, of politicians who trumpet themselves and their accomplishments, or dictators who erect statues and monuments to themselves. Their message is loud and clear: "I am great; look what I have done; I am important; pay attention to me." This is exactly the type of thing intended by the apostle. The person who parades himself is a braggart, a windbag, one who "blows his own trumpet". He calls attention to himself: his accomplishments, his wealth, his family line, etc. Such things are the antithesis of love.

The love that suffers long, that shows kindness to friends and enemies alike, that lives contentedly without envy is the same love that will not boast or brag about itself. It does not sound a fanfare before performing its righteous deeds, nor seek prominence because of its actions. It does not hire a public relations firm, or urge friends to call attention to its good works. Love is content to live and act in quietness, not letting the left hand know what the right hand is doing, not concerned with receiving praise, only with seeing that deeds are done.

A "windbag" cannot love. He is more concerned with his own self-prominence and self-promotion than with others. One scholar said,

> It is not possible to "boast" and love at the same time. The one action wants others to think highly of oneself, whether deserving or not; the other cares for none of that, but only for the good of the community as a whole.[18]

The Corinthians were scrambling for prominence; they wanted the best identification. Some said, "I am of Paul," others, "I am of Apollos" or "Cephas" or even "Christ" (1:12). They wanted gifts that could be displayed, hence their craving for the gift of tongues, rather than the quieter gifts. And they pursued these things by putting themselves on display: "Here is what I am; here is what I can do." The picture set before us is obnoxious. Love is exactly the opposite.

We must not think that we are any better than they. Do we pursue our own ways? Are we only interested in our reputations? Do we long for positions of prominence? All of these and many more are present in our lives. It would be easy for us to violate these words even in the way that we read them: "I am not like those Corinthians … How could anyone be like them?" To think in this way demonstrates just how far from the goal we really are. The sad reality in many of our churches is that we are just like them, and perhaps even more self-absorbed. Love knows nothing of self-parading and bragging. It is humble, even in what it accomplishes, because it recognizes that all good things come from above. Let us repent and ask God to work the grace of true love in us by his Spirit.

Love Is Not Puffed Up

The third phrase for our consideration, "love is not puffed up" (13:4), is a complement to the preceding phrase. It is not enough to say that love does not parade itself, it must be added that love does not allow

---

[18] Fee, *1 Corinthians*, 638.

for inflated self-opinion. Such an opinion is nothing more than air—contained for a moment, but easily released and deflated.

Once again, Paul addresses a theme that recurs throughout this epistle. In fact, of the seven times that the word is used in the New Testament, six are found in this letter.[19] It will help us to notice the other occurrences in 1 Corinthians. The first time that the word appears is at 4:6. There, Paul urges the church not to think "beyond what is written, that none of you may be puffed up on behalf of one against the other". Their arrogance was traced to their desire to identify with one or the other of the Lord's servants, neglecting the fact that they are all the same! They sought to ride on others' coat-tails, as if that gave them something more than they already had.

Later in the same chapter (4:18–19), the term appears twice more. The apostle indicates that he is determined to confront those who are puffed-up when he comes to visit them. He intended to show them real power—not just empty words. The theme continues four verses later in 5:2, where Paul diagnoses their toleration for sin. In their midst was a man guilty of a form of immorality that even Gentiles would abominate, and they were pleased with themselves! The appropriate response should have been mourning—humiliation—on their knees before God, astonished that such a thing could happen among God's people. But these Corinthians did not think in these terms. They were proud, willing to allow this man to continue in their midst. While they thought of themselves as tolerant, God's name was blasphemed among the Gentiles. What a horrible state of affairs!

The other occasion of this word is found at 8:1 which states: "Knowledge puffs up, but love edifies." As in 13:4, love is contrasted with this term, but now knowledge is diagnosed as a potential cause of pride. With our limited capacities and fallen minds, we think that

[19] The other is Colossians 2:18.

the accumulation of facts makes us better than others, but the reality is that no one knows now in the way that he ought to know and will someday know. Our present state of intellect is no basis for boasting, rather it is an indication of how much farther we have to go.

One commentator defines this word puffed up as, "inflated with its own opinion", and relates that "Napoleon always advocated the sanctity of the home and the obligation of public worship — for others. Of himself he said, 'I am not a man like other men. The laws of morality do not apply to me.'"[20] We can see what this word means: to be "big- headed", convinced of one's own importance or superiority to others. Among the Corinthians, this was demonstrated in their party divisions, their tolerance of wickedness, and their self-perceived superior knowledge. But all of it, every bit, was empty, because it lacked love.

Love is not puffed up. Was it right to be proud of party identification? In 4:7, Paul says that the only "difference" is to be attributed to God's work, and *all* of the progress is his. No one has the right to be proud—to do so is to remove God from his rightful throne and put "self" in his place. Was it right to be puffed up over immorality? Never. As we have said, the proper response would have been mourning. Was it right to be puffed up by knowledge? Certainly not. We only know in part. They were puffed up over empty, trivial and limited things. Love is not puffed up, it is humble. It cannot exaggerate its status, because it has no status apart from God's grace.

What place does arrogance have in the Christian life? The truth of 1 Corinthians 4:7 must be contemplated, in which Paul asks: "What do you have that you did not receive?" If we take inventory of our lives, we realize that everything of value that we have, literally *everything*, is a

[20] William Barclay, *The Letters to the Corinthians: New Daily Study Bible* (Philadelphia, Westminster Press, 1956), 21.

gift of God's grace and mercy. We must learn to be like John the Baptist, who said, "He must increase, but I must decrease" (John 3:30).

Christian friend, how do you view yourself and your accomplishments? Do you enjoy, even crave, praise for your actions? Do you *seek* praise for your actions? When I was a student at university, I lived for a while in a house with several other Christian young men. None of us was particularly quick to take care of the household chores, and sometimes they would go undone. To complicate matters, seldom did we notice when the tasks were completed. As a result, occasionally someone would bring attention to the work that he had done. One of the students always replied, "You have your reward!" Of course, he was seeking to be humorous, but he was also making an important point. We must not call attention to ourselves, even in our good deeds.

Are you proud of what you are, or of what you can do? Love does not parade itself; it never pushes forward for prominence. It does not envy, jealously regarding the good in someone else. Love never overestimates itself at the expense of others. Too often we major on our own minors, because we crave applause and fulfilment. Rather, we must come to realize that we are nothing, apart from the grace of God in Jesus Christ. Do you have this kind of love? Is the Spirit working this in you? Are you content, without envy, in your personal relationships? Are you humble, without self-parading or arrogance, as you relate to those around you?

May God help us to forsake ourselves, repent of our enormous sins, and by his Spirit, learn to grow in these graces.

Chapter 6
LOVE'S PROPRIETY

Love… does not behave rudely, does not seek its own…
1 Corinthians 13:4–5

We live in a world where love has become lust. We are bombarded every day with a philosophy that excuses indecency with words like consent, and promotes indulgence by the phrase, "If it feels good, do it." The apologists for modern (im)morality would have us believe that so long as two adults are "in love", their actions are legitimate. Their "love" becomes an excuse for self-gratification without commitment, and without regard for God's holy Law. We see before us a "love" that behaves rudely and seeks its own.

Sadly, it is not merely modern secular society that has exchanged love for something cheap. Too often, even among Christians, there is a tendency to allow love to be an excuse for bad behaviour and self-indulgence. The Scripture says, "love will cover a multitude of sins" (1 Pet. 4:8; cf. Prov. 10:12), but we use this as an excuse, saying, "Why won't your love cover over my sin?"

The next two qualities of love, expressed in negatives in 1 Corinthians 13:5, directly relate to our lives today. Just as they pressed on the consciences of the erring Corinthians, so we must also seek to hear the voice of the Spirit speaking in the Word of God. These things are highly relevant if we are to love as our Lord Jesus Christ loved.

Love Does Not Behave Unseemly

Our modern English translation renders Paul's words at the beginning of verse 5, love "does not behave rudely". This is a very mild translation of a distinctly strong and disparaging word. The Authorised Version is better: love "doth not behave itself unseemly". This is more sweeping. Rudeness is only part of what this word is about.

The verb used means to behave disgracefully, dishonourably, and even indecently. The family of words appears five times in the New Testament[21] with overtones of shame, especially as it relates to immorality and immodesty or indecency. It is a very sharp term with regard to the acts of love, teaching us that love, in its actions, must never degenerate into a rude, crude, unseemly decorum, without regard for its actions or consequences.

The other two occurrences in 1 Corinthians are helpful for our understanding. In 7:36, we find the word used with reference to a man's treatment "toward his virgin". The verse is notoriously difficult to interpret. Some view this section of chapter 7 as a description of father-daughter relationships, in which the father has "devoted" his daughter to the Lord from a young age, but at some point realizes that she does not have the gift of celibacy. The New American Standard Bible seems to understand the verse this way, translating the final phrase "let her marry". In this case, the improper behaviour would force her to stay unmarried against her nature and gifts, and against the express words of 7:9: "For it is better to marry than to burn with passion." Another view sees this verse with reference to the relationship sustained by a man to his fiancée. They are engaged to be married, but he holds back, perhaps for some "spiritual" reason. It may be that he was infected with the notion that marriage was less spiritual, or

[21] 1 Corinthians 7:36; 12:23; 13:5; Romans 1:27; Revelation 16:15.

perhaps even bad. In this case, Paul explains that marriage is good, and that it was very improper to act otherwise towards the promised bride. In either interpretation, the meaning of this particular word is clear; it would be a disgraceful or dishonourable act to force the woman into celibacy when such was not her gift.

A few chapters later, in chapter 12, the apostle uses the same word in a physiological sense. While discussing the church under the figure of a body, he acknowledges that there are certain parts of the human body which require modesty (12:23). They are simply not presentable. It would therefore be indecent, disgraceful, and dishonourable to be anything less than modest.

It is not surprising that Paul would use a term with such overtones when describing true love. Too often, we allow ourselves to lose a sense of propriety and decorum, and our actions become "unseemly". Certainly, this was true of the Corinthians in their relationship with the immoral man described in chapter 5. One is able to imagine their boasting of love to this man—they maybe did not approve of his actions but thought that their love for him could overcome his grotesque lifestyle. They were wrong; their love was quite "unseemly".

Paul, in using this term, is not speaking only of lust or immorality or immodesty—though surely these ideas are present. Here, he presents us with a love that must *always* behave properly in its actions. This is well illustrated by noting the words of 1 Corinthians 11:17–22. The problem present among the Corinthians is obvious there. A meal, sometimes called a "love-feast", was held by the members of the assembly. Instead of being a wonderful time of friendship and encouragement, it degenerated into a disgusting show of rude and unseemly behaviour. There was no sense of Christian love, instead there was jostling for position ("each one takes his own supper ahead of others", 11:21), hunger, and even drunkenness! Some feasted while others had little or nothing. Such acts shock us.

Love does not behave unseemly. It has a due sense of what is appropriate; it weighs the benefits for others; it understands the sensitivities of the situation, and presents itself always with modesty and propriety. Love is gracious.

We come face to face with our own sins as we contemplate these words. There are many circumstances in which we fail to express the kind of love Christ would have us show. We do the very things that Paul says are the opposite of true love. How do you respond to personal inconvenience, especially when caused by someone else's mistake? Do you grumble and complain, perhaps carrying on in front of your spouse and children, or co-workers? Or for example, how would you feel about a policeman who stopped you and gave you a summons for an infringement of the driving laws? Many of us would have improper thoughts in our minds, even if we are guilty of breaking the traffic law! We may think: "Why did he stop me? Lots of others get away with this." How foolish of us, and how sad—since the all-seeing God knows our very thoughts. The policeman sees a calm face, the Lord sees a boiling heart.

Love does not behave unseemly. If you would love, you must learn to handle properly all of life's situations, from its rebukes to its inconveniences. Our conduct in all things must show forth love. "It is well said that you can spot a gentleman not by the way he addresses his king, but by the way he addresses his servants."[22]

Love Does Not Seek Its Own

This phrase is very plain, but it deserves careful attention. In the line of qualities, this may be the key. It is obvious, based on what we have

[22] Carson, *Showing the Spirit,* 62.

learned thus far, that love cannot be selfish. Now Paul states this openly and directly. Love does not centre on *me*, on what *I* think or want or do. It realizes that I am not the centre of the universe; that the world does not revolve around me. My ideas are not the most important; my desires must not take priority.

There are two things to notice in Paul's words. In the first place, he employs a verb of urgency: to seek. The word implies a diligent search and even a demand, with the centre of attention on the desires of the individual. It involves consistent, concerted effort, the demands of time and energy associated with a quest. In the second place, he uses a somewhat indefinite term, "its own things", to describe the object of the search. By using these words, he addresses the perception of possession, and even entitlement, present in the mind of the one described. Most likely, he intends the words to refer to "interests". It could mean either, "Love does not seek its own interests", or perhaps, "Love does not seek itself." In either case, love does not centre on itself. "Love is not preoccupied with its own things, but with the interests of others."[23]

True love will not give its time and effort to self-satisfaction; it realizes its own limits, and refuses to chase after the sinful. Once again, as we consider this epistle, we see that the Corinthians knew little of this. They clamoured for self-gratification, constantly seeking their own things. Each one wanted the highest prominence, or the best party-identification, or the most spectacular gifts, planning for themselves, politicking for themselves, putting themselves in front of others. Paul emphasizes that love must look outward, not inward. Only a few chapters before (10:24, 32–33), he had said,

> Let no one seek his own, but each one the other's well-being …
> Give no offence, either to the Jews or to the Greeks or to the

[23] MacArthur, *1 Corinthians*, 345.

> church of God, just as I also please all men in all things, not seeking my own profit, but the profit of many, that they may be saved.

Whether the issue is curtailing its liberty, or giving up its prominence, or rejoicing in someone else's gift, love does not seek its own. It refuses to set out on the quest of self- fulfilment, and "It is prepared to give up for the sake of others even what it is entitled to."[24] This is the heart of the issue. Is this a description of your love?

It might be good to return to the gospel for help and illumination. When our teacher, Paul, sought to address another church about this matter, he wrote of Christ:

> Let this mind be in you which was also in Christ Jesus, who, being in the form of God, did not consider it robbery to be equal with God, but made Himself of no reputation, taking the form of a bondservant, and coming in the likeness of men. And being found in appearance as a man, He humbled Himself and became obedient to the point of death, even the death of the cross. (Phil. 2:5–8)

By right, Jesus Christ, the second person of the holy Trinity, deserved all of the praise of heaven and earth. Yet he put this aside and, in obedience to his Father and out of love for his people, took the lowest possible station—the place of a servant. And he did this, knowing that the end would be a gruesome death on a cross. Even more profoundly, he knew that that death would involve enduring the wrath of God poured out on sin. How astounding is this? The rightful heir of heaven freely and gladly humbled himself, and he did this for the sake of his

[24] C. K. Barrett, quoted in Carson, *Showing the Spirit*, 62.

enemies—sinful women and men, like you and me. This is true love—all that we are and all that we have must be found here at Christ's cross. When we contemplate our Lord, we understand what selfless love is about, and we find help to see it grow in our own lives.

Who, or what, do you love? And why? Many Americans of my generation will remember the words spoken by President Kennedy at his inauguration in 1961: "Ask not what your country can do for you; ask what you can do for your country." A true patriot understands these words; they reflect Paul's principle, on a national level. Love does not seek what can be done for itself but does what it can for others.

Do you love your spouse? Is it for what you can do for her or him, or for what she or he may do for you?

Do you love your church? Does your love depend on what the church does for you, or on what you can freely do for the church?

Why do you love what you love? This can be a painful question, but it is exactly what Paul intends. If we would love, we must be truly outward-looking. Sadly, for many Christians, this is a great problem. Our apostle himself said, "For all seek their own, not the things which are of Christ Jesus" (Phil. 2:21). The language is almost identical —what a terrible indictment to make. But it is true; many Christians live for themselves. We are taken up with ourselves. We begin and end most of our days with ourselves at the centre of our world. O that God would grant us repentance!

John MacArthur records an inscription on a tombstone in a small English village. It reads:

> Here lies a miser who lived for himself,
> and cared for nothing but gathering wealth.
> Now where he is or how he fares,
> nobody knows and nobody cares.

Then he mentions a plain tombstone at St Paul's Cathedral in London which reads,

> Sacred to the memory of General Charles George Gordon, who at all times and everywhere gave his strength to the weak, his substance to the poor, his sympathy to the suffering, his heart to God.[25]

What will be your epitaph when you die? May God help us to look to Christ, learn from and lean on him.

[25] MacArthur, 1 Corinthians, 344.

Chapter 7
THE TEMPER OF LOVE

Love… is not provoked, thinks no evil…
1 Corinthians 13:4–5

Consider, if you will, a husband and wife, married for several years. Patterns of behaviour have had plenty of time to develop into the routine of every day. He is a man with a temper. While most acquaintances, especially church folks, have never seen his anger, his wife knows it very well. Too often, he allows his irritation to bubble over, either at his wife or in her presence. When the supper is late, or the car needs expensive repairs, or the chequebook will not balance, he fumes, and his wife must bear the brunt of his infuriation.

She resents his outbursts. While they were dating, she seldom saw this aspect of the man, for he was able to mask the anger in various situations. But, after the wedding, he began to let down his guard and give rein to his unholy emotion. As the pattern developed, she felt more and more bitterness because of her husband's displays. While others saw him as a fine example of Christian morality, she had to live with the reality of short fuses and sudden outbursts. She remembers most of the situations in which her husband has given vent to his furies. Often, it has been for small inconveniences or petty problems, when she sees how unreasonable and unchristian her husband is. So, she resents his temper, and to some degree holds this against him.

Do these two love each other? Probably in many areas, but not in this matter. Both are guilty of violating the nature of true love. Paul's next two phrases focus in on the problems of this man and wife, and probably the rest of us as well.

Love Is Not Provoked

As the apostle continues to teach us about love, he addresses a similar issue to one already noted, that love suffers long. But he is not merely repeating this idea for emphasis; rather he wants us to consider another side of the beautiful fulness of love. There is more to the matter than has been said.

What does it mean to be provoked? The word itself was a medical term, used to describe the high point of a fever. Sometimes it carried the sense *to sharpen* or *bring to a point*, and was often used with as a metaphor, *rouse to anger*. We find the family of words used several times in the New Testament.

Occasionally, the word was used positively. In Hebrews 10:24, we find a very striking phrase, translated in the Authorised Version as "Let us consider one another to provoke unto love and to good works." What an interesting expression: provoke to love! The idea is intended to capture our attention. Believers ought to seek ways to sharpen love and good works among each other. Luke also uses the verbal form of the word positively in Acts 17:16. In that text, he describes Paul's response to the idolatry and paganism of Greece. As a Christian, walking through the heart of the city devoted to Greek philosophy, he was sickened by the religious climate around him. He was provoked—what other response could a sensitive believer's soul give to such overt unbelief? Here was the fountain of all sorts of damning doctrines, placed on display everywhere. Paul longed for Jesus Christ to be worshipped, and for the pagan idols to be destroyed.

He was provoked, and responded by preaching the gospel to all who would listen.

Perhaps more directly related to our exposition is Luke's use of the word to describe a sad incident in Acts 15: 36–40. There we find the account of a serious disagreement between Paul and his companion Barnabas. As they prepared to visit the cities where churches had been planted, Barnabas "was determined to take with them John called Mark" (15:37). Paul disagreed, because John Mark had departed from them on a previous mission. Luke's words are very clear: "the contention became so sharp that they parted from one another" (15:39). Barnabas took Mark and went one way; Paul chose Silas and went another. The language used is very strong, the disagreement profound. Who was right? From our perspective it is difficult to judge. It is clear that God blessed Paul's ministry, but it is just as apparent that God blessed Barnabas's ministry, and John Mark's life as well, for Paul himself speaks of both (Col. 4:10; 2 Tim. 4:11). While the results may not have been bad, the quarrel itself was not good.

The only other place in the New Testament where this family of words appears is at 1 Corinthians 13:5. One commentator has an interesting remark:

> Paul was a vehement character, inclined to strong reactions and particularly sensitive to what he considered disloyalty or laggard response to his leadership. Love, he writes in 1 Corinthians. 13:5, perhaps a little self-reproachfully, "is not easily provoked", and he uses the verb [of the same family].[26]

Did Paul write from his own experience in 1 Corinthians 13:5? One

[26] E. M. Blaiklock, *The Acts of the Apostles: An Historical Commentary* (Grand Rapids: Eerdmans, 1959), 118-19.

wonders, is it a characteristic of great men, great leaders, that they often disdain others who cannot fully agree with them, or want to pursue another course? Great men can and do fall, and perhaps this is an area especially liable to be a snare. We remember Jesus' disciples, who were jealous of those who "cast out demons in Jesus" name" but did not follow them. Jesus' rebuke was straightforward: "'Do not forbid him … he who is not against us is on our side'" (Mark 9:39–41). Are leaders sometimes so convinced of their own calling and rightness that they cannot conceive that someone might have a different opinion, or that they themselves might be wrong?

Love is not provoked. The word speaks of contention and even anger, the response of emotion to an unwanted or unexpected situation, and Paul says that it is foreign to love.

What then does he want us to understand here? It is this—in our personal relationships, there must be care for the expression of our emotions. Have you ever heard the phrase, "You always hurt the ones you love"? There is more truth in these words than we like to admit. While we want to present ourselves to the world as respectable and controlled, we are less careful at home. In the intimacy of our personal relationships, the wall of appearance is removed and we show ourselves as we really are. Once we have begun to express our sinfulness, we continue to do so. Each time is easier, until we forget about loving those who should be closest, while we keep up appearances to those on the outside.

Have you ever been involved in a heated discussion at home, when suddenly the telephone rings? How does it get answered? Almost always, we control our emotions so that they are disguised to the one calling. He does not know that a moment before, our voice was raised and our face was red with anger. We have provoked our loved ones but hidden this fact from the caller.

This is the problem of the husband we met a few pages ago. Over the years, he has indulged an angry response to the inconveniences and aggravations of life—but he has done so in a constrained way. In the presence of most people, he is a model of self-control. But before the ones he loves the most, he lets loose with unchristian behaviour. His wife must endure his tirades, and her esteem for him lowers with each outburst.

Really, this kind of provocation is self-centred. We think that our own plans, desires, and opinions must have priority over everyone else, and when something gets in the way, the result is sinful anger. We may be able to hide it from many eyes, but not with those closest to us. Have you fallen into this kind of behaviour? Have you asked your loved ones to forgive you?

Love Thinks No Evil

Provocation does happen. How is one to respond, when genuine injury is given? What does Paul press upon the Corinthians? His next phrase teaches us what to think and how to act.

Love lives in a fallen world, surrounded by offences. It is constantly perplexed by fear, hatred, and sorrow. Often it will be assaulted for its purity, ridiculed for honesty, and slandered for righteousness. As the blows are received, love acts in a certain way, a way different from the world and its responses to the same deeds.

For the wife in our mythical couple, trouble comes through her husband's carnal outbursts. When he sputters and fumes, she cringes in reply, remembering the frequent times in the past when he has indulged this behaviour. For her, each instance is another log placed on the smouldering fire of resentment. She remembers and contemplates the wrongs done in her presence. As a result of their acts, their marital love is often cool, and sometimes nearly extinguished.

For most of us, a mental record of the wrongs done to us is very important. We keep an account sheet, fed by long memories of misdeeds. But when we do this, we turn away from love. The apostle's words move us in a different direction. A quick reading of the English phrase "thinks no evil" (13:5) might cause us to misunderstand the intention of the text. Perhaps a more direct translation might be "Love keeps no account of evil" or "Love maintains no record book of wrongs done." The "evil" is plainly anything that is not good, right, and holy. But the verb rendered "think" does not merely refer to mental activity, but rather to the keeping of accounts. It was a word used by bookkeepers when they entered figures in a ledger. They made permanent records, and these could be consulted whenever necessary. It can also refer to the practice of keeping a journal of facts and figures; like keeping a careful record in our chequebooks—all of the entries dated, tallied and checked against the monthly bank statement.

In fact, the New Testament uses this word abundantly with this sense. In Romans, the apostle frequently employs it to speak of reckoning (Rom. 4:3–4, 6, 8–11, 24), as if God were a bookkeeper of righteousness, and maintained records of these men of faith. In the gospel, our sins are reckoned, imputed to Christ, and his righteousness is imputed to us. This is the great doctrine of our faith. We receive the benefits of his active obedience—his life of holy law-keeping; and of his passive obedience—his life of suffering, culminating in his death on the cross. We are saved by Christ alone.

When we see the word in this light, its meaning is clarified for us. While love may suffer many things, it never enters these things into a "mental ledger", so that it remembers and meditates on the wrongs and injustices it has received. One author has said,

> Love "keeps no record of wrongs", a private file of personal grievances that can be consulted and nursed whenever there is possibility of some new slight. Its stance in the presence of genuine evil precludes such accounting.[27]

Another has stated,

> Resentment is careful to keep books, which it reads and rereads, hoping for a chance to get even. Love keeps no books, because it has no place for resentment or grudges. Chrysostom observed that a wrong done against love is like a spark that falls into the sea and is quenched. Love quenches wrongs rather than records them. It does not cultivate memories out of evil.[28]

To phrase this differently, love forgives and forgets. Love really seeks to put away the evil—it has been done, let that be the end of it. Nursing the grudge, marking the record in one's "sin account book" only allows the evil to fester and again show its wickedness. Sin must be mortified, killed, and that means that we must kill it, even when we bear the brunt of its wickedness.

The apostle Peter understood this point well and spoke about it at length. Listen to his words:

> Servants, be submissive to your masters with all fear, not only to the good and gentle, but also to the harsh. For this is commendable, if because of conscience toward God one endures grief, suffering wrongfully. For what credit is it if, when you are beaten for your faults, you take it patiently? But

[27] Carson, *Showing the Spirit*, 62.
[28] MacArthur, *1 Corinthians*, 347.

when you do good and suffer, if you take it patiently, this is commendable before God. For to this you were called, because Christ also suffered for us, leaving us an example, that you should follow His steps:

"Who committed no sin,
Nor was deceit found in his mouth";

who, when He was reviled, did not revile in return; when He suffered, He did not threaten, but committed Himself to Him who judges righteously; who Himself bore our sins in His own body on the tree, that we, having died to sins, might live for righteousness—by whose stripes you were healed. (1 Pet. 2:18-24)

Finally, all of you be of one mind, having compassion for one another; love as brothers, be tender-hearted, be courteous; not returning evil for evil or reviling for reviling, but on the contrary blessing, knowing that you were called to this, that you may inherit a blessing. For

"He who would love life
And see good days,
Let him refrain his tongue from evil,
And his lips from speaking deceit.
Let him turn away from evil and do good;
Let him seek peace and pursue it.
For the eyes of the LORD are on the righteous,
And His ears are open to their prayers;
But the face of the LORD is against those who do evil"
(1 Pet. 3:8–12)

As those who have received the blessings of the gospel, let us bear Christ's image and love as he did. There is no place for record-keeping.

Dear friend, please ask yourself this question: "Against whom do I hold a record of wrongs?" Probably most of us have some mental account book. We all have been on the receiving end of offences and injustices. There is no excuse for the sins others have committed against us. Yet, we are not to hold these acts against them. Let the "spark fall into the sea"; without the ocean of forgiveness, you may erect a structure of dry tinder, even a little spark can cause a great flame. Forgive and forget every offence against you; just as God has done with you.

Do you remember our husband and wife? They did love each other, but at the points we mentioned, they failed to love. He gave free rein to his temper, she held it against him, mentally recording each occurrence. They are headed for danger, for if they continue to leave these things unchecked, they may find that a serious breach has developed. Please don't be like them. Don't let your love be provoked in your relationships. Don't keep a list of grievances. May God help us to seek after the gentle spirit of Christ, and his ocean of forgiveness.

Chapter 8
LOVE'S HAPPINESS

Love… does not rejoice in iniquity, but rejoices in the truth…
1 Corinthians 13:4, 6

When I first began to consider verse 6, it almost seemed that these words were so self-evident they did not need to be stated. Why would Paul include such an obvious truth, in such a profound passage? Isn't it plain that love does not and cannot rejoice in iniquity? Who would ever make the mistake of confusing true love with the enjoyment of sin?

But as I read the comments of others, the meaning and importance of this phrase began to be clear. Let us notice the words of Lewis Smedes, as he begins his own comments on these words:

> Could it be that we all really do rejoice in evil? Perhaps rejoicing in evil is in fact the norm, not the exception, and that *not* rejoicing in evil is so difficult for us that only the power of God's love can get us to hate evil?…
>
> We *do* rejoice in evil, even if we do not scream "Bravo!" at every mean and sordid sin. All it takes to rejoice in evil is to approve of its being here, to be content that we have some evil around, to endorse its presence in our world. We may even regret most

> of the evil in the world—especially that which hurts us—but we do rejoice in evil if we approve any of [it] at all.[29]

Smedes has put his finger on the problem. Paul does not merely state the obvious. Rather, he opens up to us a new perspective on our lives. Perhaps we need to hear these words more than we might realize. Do you ever rejoice in iniquity?

Love Does Not Rejoice in Iniquity

This is the last of the negatives describing love, and it is coupled with a positive statement, so that we might see the full story of this aspect of love. Each of the previous phrases implies a positive; here it is stated explicitly.

The words used by Paul are plain. To rejoice is to be happy; iniquity is unrighteousness. The latter is the generic term for anything that comes short of the holiness of God's character. Together, the words imply gladness in any occurrence of sin; to tolerate, encourage or enjoy evil, in any and all of its forms. It may be as grotesque as murder or as simple as gossip, but it is openly or secretly willing to allow the presence and existence of evil.

We have already noticed the incident of the man involved in terrible immorality as reported in 1 Corinthians 5. Here was an incident in which the Corinthians rejoiced in iniquity. Paul is not necessarily saying that they took delight in the man's sin, simply that they failed to "mourn" and did not enact the discipline due such wickedness.

Once again, the apostle's words are directly applicable to his original readers; but they also must be heard by us.It may be that, like the Corinthians, there are forms of iniquity that we rejoice in. Of

[29] Lewis Smedes, *Love Within Limits: Realizing Selfless Love in a Selfish World* (Grand Rapids: Eerdmans, 1978), 81.

course, we should never take delight in overt evil—as the Corinthians did, growing puffed up, proud of their toleration of immorality. But there are many subtle ways in which we may be guilty of the same sin. For instance, sometimes we rejoice when our enemies suffer evil. In November 1979, the United States embassy in Teheran, Iran, was occupied by insurgents, and 52 American citizens were held hostage for 444 days. Many were outraged by this act. But when, on 3 July 1988, a commercial Iranian airliner was shot down by a US Navy missile, we chalk it up to the dangers of war, and secretly gloat that "they got what they deserved". Closer to home, we may have the same attitude in interpersonal relationships. We allow jealousy to rage in our hearts, and we are glad when we see someone we don't like suffer. It may be only a petty difficulty, but we take quiet delight in their trouble.

Most frequently, our tongues betray our delight in evil. This can be summarized in one word: gossip. An author has written:

> One of the most common forms of rejoicing in sin is gossip. Gossips would do little harm if they did not have so many eager listeners. This sin, which many Christians treat lightly, is wicked not only because it uncaringly reveals the weaknesses and sins of others, and therefore hurts rather than helps them, but because the heart of gossip is rejoicing in evil. Gossip that is true is still gossip... It has been defined as a vice enjoyed vicariously. The essence of gossip is gloating over the shortcomings and sins of others.[30]

This correctly diagnoses a great evil, yet one that is all too common among Christians. Under the guise of caring for someone's well-being, we talk about their sins; we may even take "pleasure" in being the first

[30] MacArthur, *1 Corinthians*, 350.

to spread the news. We may secretly gloat that we have kept ourselves from that sin. What we are doing is rejoicing in evil. Examine how you talk about others. What do you say on the telephone? Over the back fence? At the barbershop? At the dinner table? In your elders' meetings?

Love seeks to cast these things away; true love wants no part in any manifestation of evil. It requires the determination, by the grace of God, to put aside natural delight in evil and pursue righteousness.

Love Rejoices in the Truth

Truth is the complementing grace to love. A glance at the English translation seems to indicate that Paul uses the same verb in both parts of the verse, but this is not correct. In the second half, he uses a compound form of the word, adding a prefix to the earlier term. This new word means something like "shared joy". It is used a few verses earlier, at 12:26, which says, "If one member is honoured, all the members rejoice with it." This is the heightened joy of a group expressing their delight together. Perhaps a good illustration would be the exuberance of the guests at a wedding reception. Every one of them expresses gladness at the happy occasion. The kind of rejoicing described here is not so much an individual experience as it is a mutual delight.

Truth is that which reflects the character of the God who *is* truth. It is not a philosophical concept nor an abstract postulation, but a real entity, reflecting the holiness of God. Love finds great joy in the truth, but it does not do so in isolation. Truth is so wonderful, so beautiful in its reflection of God's majesty, that every follower must join in the enjoyment.

But there is something unexpected here. Why does Paul contrast iniquity with truth? One might expect righteousness to correspond with unrighteousness. What is the apostle seeking to teach us?

The reason for this contrast rests in the very nature of truth. Consider, for example, the words of the Lord Jesus Christ:

> He who speaks from himself seeks his own glory; but He who seeks the glory of the One who sent Him is true, and no unrighteousness is in Him. (John 7:18)

In speaking of himself, Jesus makes the same contrast as Paul. The Jews wondered at his understanding and sought to come to some conclusions about his identity. Some thought that he was a good man, while others said that he was a deceiver (7:12). Knowing that there was great debate over his exact nature, the Lord spoke to them, directing their attention heavenward. His mission was authorized by God himself—it was true, and thus there could be no wickedness in him. His identity must be understood in terms of his mission. Sadly, the people did not respond as they ought, and accused him of being demon-possessed. His point is well made though. Truth is antithetical to unrighteousness.

In a completely different context, Paul employs the same kind of language:

> The wrath of God is revealed from heaven against all ungodliness and unrighteousness of men, who suppress the truth in unrighteousness. (Rom. 1:18)

This verse is only a short portion of Romans 1, the most disturbing delineation of the depths of wickedness found in the Word of God. Paul diagnoses the utter antipathy sinners have toward God—they will pursue sin whenever possible, and use whatever means are at their disposal to "suppress" the truth. Fallen men cannot abide truth;

it exposes them as they really are and reveals the terrible reality of the judgements they face. While creation cries out of the being and power of God, reminding men of their evil ways, they do everything within their power to bury the truth. It is the bright spotlight exposing their sin.

As Paul continues his argument, he makes a similar point:

> [God will render] to those who are self-seeking and do not obey the truth, but obey unrighteousness—indignation and wrath. (Rom. 2:8)

Notice that truth must be obeyed. As we have said, it is not merely a philosophical construct, to satisfy the inquiring minds of deep thinkers. Truth carries with it obligations. Unrighteousness is opposed to truth because neither truth nor error is morally neutral. Truth is verbalized righteousness, and error is a defection from everything that is morally good. Truth complements righteousness, error opposes it. When the Psalmist writes, "The fool has said in his heart, 'There is no God,'" (Ps. 14:1a) he is not merely speaking of a silly man. The word "fool" in the Old Testament often implies someone who is morally corrupt. His denial of God is a moral act—because his conscience cannot abide the thought of a holy, absolute, and sovereign being before whom he will stand in judgement. He believes that it is better to deny the existence of God than to think of facing him.

Why does the modern scientific community reject the Bible's account of creation? Is it simply from scientific observation and fact gathering? Not at all. At its root, it is the outworking of a godless philosophy, which would rather deny God than acknowledge him. The geneticist Francis Crick contended that man is just a sophisticated machine; if man is simply the result of genetic mutations, kicked up from primordial slime, there can be no definite morality. In my own lifetime, I have witnessed physicians, theoretically devoted to the Hippocratic Oath, performing abortions and supporting euthanasia. The cause is a rejection of truth. When God is removed from moral equations, when truth is not final, nothing remains but the survival of the fittest.

The same is true in religion. One generation's heterodoxy becomes the next generation's heresy, and even justification for sin. Multiple examples could be given. For instance, in nineteenth-century New England, Unitarianism vied for a place as a respectable Christian expression of faith. Its champions argued for its tenets based on Scripture and reason, and in some cases it at least faintly resembled evangelical orthodoxy. Today, it has no resemblance at all, nor does it seek such. The leading "churches" from the movement are notorious for their promotion of pluralism, and advocacy of the most notorious sins—even the types of sin described by Paul in Romans 1. Is it any surprise that this has happened? It should not be. Deviation from the truth, when left uncorrected, always leads to moral error.

Love exults in the truth; it relishes and longs for that which is true. Love desires to think God's thoughts and to walk in his ways, understanding that the beauty of truth is in its holiness.

Why are these things important? Why must we learn them? Because the power of sin is so strong that it pulls us often into error. Truth *always* promotes righteousness; error is *always* associated with evil. This theme is repeated throughout the Scriptures. Jesus Christ is the truth, and his way is the way of righteousness.

Do you know and love the truth? Are you seeking to reject every form of iniquity and delighting in what is true? Do you profit from the preaching of the Word of God? Do you see truth working in you, rejecting sin and pursuing holiness? This is what truth does—it works toward righteousness. Dear friend, I urge you to hear God's Word, grow in your love for it, and rejoice as it changes you.

Pastor, your task is to proclaim this word. It alone is the instrument employed by the Spirit to bring holiness into the lives of your hearers. Study hard and teach your people the whole counsel of God. Remember Paul's exhortation to Timothy: "Preach the Word!" (2 Tim. 4:2). As you do this, they will become more and more like the living word, Jesus Christ. As Paul reminds us, rejoicing is a corporate activity. When your people leave worship, make certain that they are rejoicing to have heard the voice of the Saviour in the preaching of his word.

The most powerful means of putting away the bad is to put in the good. May God help us to rejoice in the truth.

Chapter 9
LOVE AND ALL THINGS

Love… bears all things, believes all things,
hopes all things, endures all things.
1 Corinthians 13:4, 7

The Corinthian church was riddled with problems, all stemming from defects in their theology which caused faulty behaviour. One of the most basic errors came from a misunderstanding the teaching about the coming of the kingdom of God, used as an excuse for both laxity and arrogance, which marked their failure to love.

Paul taught, as did Jesus, that with the coming of Christ, the kingdom of heaven had invaded the realm of men. Both emphasized that Christians do not merely look forward to a future kingdom of bliss but right now enter the rule of God in Christ. Jesus is Lord *now*, actively subduing his enemies, making them a footstool for his feet (Ps. 110:1). However, all the varied blessings of his rule are still yet to be fully realised.

The Corinthians understood the doctrine of Christ's lordship but carried it beyond the teaching of Paul and Jesus. They began to act as if the kingdom of Christ had already come in its final form. Rather than waiting, they wanted to enjoy all of the blessings and dominion of that kingdom here and now. They lived as entitled heirs of the kingdom, exercising its rights and privileges. Unfortunately, they failed to recognize that the invasion of the kingdom was spiritual, not material, and that they were acting in a way not appropriate for kingdom citizens.

1 Corinthians 13 is a brilliant corrective to their error. Paul seeks to remind them that although the kingdom has come and is coming, they continue to live in a fallen world. They are still sinners, subject to the sinful acts of others. They must learn to live the life of Christ's kingdom in such a context—not seize the blessings for themselves now. The means of doing so is love—a love which willingly overlooks and forgives the sins of others while seeking to mortify its own. In order to understand his argument, we must consider his language very carefully. If love is to bear, believe, hope, and endure *all things*, there is much to cover!

All Things

To begin, let us look at the category that Paul is using to make his point. Four times in verse 7, Paul uses the phrase "all things"— love "bears all things, believes all things, hopes all things, endures all things." It is vital that we understand the significance of this phrase in the flow of the apostle's thought. It is not simply a catch-all phrase, as it might be in our own conversation: "What's wrong with your car?" "Everything." In the New Testament, it has a very specific and special meaning. It occurs frequently throughout the Bible, and especially in 1 Corinthians, where Paul uses it to counter the false theology present in the church.

We should notice two key texts in the epistle. Firstly, in 1 Corinthians 8:1–6, we find a clear statement of the sovereignty of God, and of the relationship of "all things" to him. Notice what is said there:

> Now concerning things offered to idols: We know that we all have knowledge. Knowledge puffs up, but love edifies. And if anyone thinks that he knows anything, he knows nothing yet as he ought to know. But if anyone loves God, this one is known by Him.
>
> Therefore concerning the eating of things offered to idols, we know that an idol is nothing in the world, and that there is no other God but one. For even if there are so-called gods, whether in heaven or on earth (as there are many gods and many lords), yet for us there is one God, the Father, of whom are all things, and we for Him; and one Lord Jesus Christ, through whom are all things, and through whom we live.

The question of idols was a pressing concern in the confusion of pagan deities of the Mediterranean world. Paul addresses this matter, asserting that idols are literally nothing—they are empty and vain. In contrast, the one true God exists in heaven, and rules in sovereign dominion.

Paul expresses this by using our phrase two times. In the first case, God is the creator of "all things". Whatever exists, exists because God himself has called it into being. Here, "all things" refers to creation in its entirety—everything has been called into existence by God. To worship an idol is to place a created entity in God's position—a violation of the created order. Even men, the crown of creation, exist for God, and not vice versa.

In the second case, we read that Jesus Christ sustains "all things". Not only does everything have its source in God, but also its sustenance. Christ upholds "all things by the word of His power" (Heb. 1:3). "In Him we live and move and have our being…" (Acts 17:28).

The triune God directly rules creation.

Colossians 1:16–17 expresses this truth well:

> For by [Christ] all things were created that are in heaven and that are on earth, visible and invisible, whether thrones or dominions or principalities or powers. All things were created through Him and for Him. And He is before all things, and in Him all things consist.

"All things" is a creation category. It makes us realize that God has caused all of the created universe to be woven together as the tapestry of his eternal plan.

Secondly, let us notice 1 Corinthians 15:27–28:

> For "He has put all things under His feet." But when He says "all things are put under Him," it is evident that He who put all things under Him is excepted. Now when all things are made subject to Him, then the Son Himself will also be subject to Him who put all things under Him, that God may be all in all.

The citation, "He has put all things under His feet," is from Psalm 8, an inspired poem looking back on creation in all of its beauty and glory. Not only do the words "all things" look back to creation, and around at the present, but as Paul looks to the future, he sees all of the strands of God's tapestry brought together as one. In the past, Adam was created to be God's vicegerent, ruling over all of this marvellous world. He lost his lordship when he fell, but it is now restored to man in Jesus Christ. In the future restoration, "all things" will find their consummation in him.

What impression do we get from these verses? Plainly, God is sovereign in "all things", past, present, and future. However, while "all things" are of God, *presently* "all things" do not reflect the perfect completed plan of God. The circumstances of the present are not identical to the circumstances of the future. And the Corinthians failed to understand this point.

The Corinthian Error

The Corinthians took this doctrine of final consummation and misapplied it in their own situation. Their error was a failure to comprehend the difference between then and now; between the present condition of believers living in a fallen world, and the future condition of living in a perfect world.

There are many verses that make this abundantly clear; we shall notice two. In 1 Corinthians 6:12, we read, "All things are lawful for me, but all things are not helpful. All things are lawful for me, but I will not be brought under the power of any." "All things are lawful" may have been the boast of some (or many) in the church. They seem to have thought along these lines: "If Christ is Lord of all things, then I can lawfully use them as I will!" In 10:23, Paul repeats the refrain: "All things are lawful for me, but not all things are helpful; all things are lawful for me, but not all things edify." As in 1 Corinthians 13:7, "all things" is used four times. Their slogan, "all things are lawful," was essentially an excuse for misbehaviour. They wanted to enjoy "all things"—all the pleasures of life—in the here and now. And this completely undermined any genuine expression of love, for it became utterly self-centred. While it is absolutely true that Jesus Christ is Lord of all things, that does not mean that all things are as they ought to be or can be enjoyed in the immediate. The perfection of the kingdom of God is as yet a future state, while the Corinthians lived as if it were already present!

The corrective for their error was a proper understanding of the difference between *creation* and *consummation*. They treated the *creation* of all things as if they were the *consummation* of all things, failing to reckon with the ongoing contradictions with sin and evil and sorrow in this world. They believed that, as all things were created as good, they could all be used by them as they pleased. Yet since Adam, the world and everything in it is fallen and does not reflect the full perfection of God. For this reason, it may only be used with wisdom. Paul does not argue the unlawfulness of "all things" but rather the wise use of them. Something may be lawful, but also be unhelpful or unwise in its use. For instance, it is lawful to eat, but only in moderation.

The Corinthians were so "heavenly minded that they were no earthly good". They wanted to live as if the "all things" of eternity were already in place in their lives, and thus they fell prey to a false super-spirituality that permitted the very things it should have prevented—all forms of immorality and selfishness. Paul's words in 3:21–23 are especially appropriate:

> …For all things are yours: whether Paul or Apollos or Cephas, or the world or life or death, or things present or things to come—all are yours. And you are Christ's, and Christ is God's.

This is the lesson: all things *are* yours, but you belong to Christ, awaiting the final phase of his kingdom. Therefore, you must live with the tension of a fallen world, while waiting for the "all things" of eternity.

Love and All Things

What does love have to do with all things? Notice what Paul says in 13:7: "Love bears all things, believes all things, hopes all things, endures all things." In each case, he employs the creation sense of the term, including everything in a fallen, imperfect world. Love must act appropriate to its present condition, not some perfect future state. Even more to the point, "all things" modifies each verb, taking it up another notch.

1. *Love bears all things*. Literally, love puts up with all things—even all fallen things. It lives with whatever comes its way: uncomfortable situations, inconveniences, difficulties. Love protects exposure to wrongs, refuses to disclose indignities suffered.
2. *Love believes all things*. "Believes" here probably should be understood in the sense of "faithful", or "keeps faith". We are not to think that Paul teaches us that love is gullible; rather, he is saying that love's faith never gives up. It holds onto Christ in every situation and trusts in his sovereignty even when "all things" may seem otherwise. In a fallen world, faith working through love (Gal. 5:6) brings forth holiness to the glory of God. The lives of every one of God's people (see Heb. 11) make this point. Though the world seems wrong, we have faith that Christ is Lord.
3. *Love hopes all things*. Hope in the Bible is often used very differently from the way that we use this word in modern English. We equate hope with wishing: "I hope it doesn't rain tomorrow." To the contrary, in the Scriptures it refers to firm confidence. The author of the letter to the Hebrews calls it "an anchor of the soul" (6:19)—hardly a qualification for a wish! Love's hope depends on the certainty of Christ in all things, whatever may be the state of a fallen world.
4. *Love endures all things*. This is perseverance. Love has a tenacity in the present, based on its knowledge of the future, to endure every circumstance. Because it is rooted in Christ, it is able, even in a

> fallen world, to press ahead, knowing that all of the promises of the word of God are true. It may need to empty itself of all of its goods and give its body to be burned (1 Corinthians 13: 2), but it is willing to do so.

Now compare this with the Corinthians. They were exactly the opposite. They were anything but longsuffering and kind; they were envious, parading, puffed-up, rude, self-seeking, provocative, evil-thinking, rejoicing in iniquity, and not rejoicing in truth.

Their boast was “all things”, but their complete misunderstanding of the difference between *now* and *then* caused them to live with a faulty view of the Christian faith. They viewed themselves as lords and conquerors, not as servants and endurers. Martin Luther would say that they lived with a theology of glory, and not with a theology of the cross. To put it simply, the church militant is not the church triumphant. Paul must use their favourite phrase, “all things”, and show them what love does with it—serve Christ and others in love.

What about you? Do you have a false view of “all things” which affects the life you live? We do not live in a perfect world, we are not perfect people; we are sinners and we live with sinners. God’s call to us is to learn to endure—to bear, believe and hope—to love as Christ loved and loves.

In what area of your life does a super-spiritual excuse allow you to salve your conscience with false relief? Do you indulge your flesh or excuse your sin as they did? Are you a Corinthian Christian or an enduring Christian?

May God help us to learn, as did the Corinthians, to show this kind of love—bearing and enduring, believing and hoping, with one another, with Christ, with all things.

Chapter 10
LOVE'S PERMANENCE

Love never fails. But whether there are prophecies, they will fail; whether there are tongues, they will cease; whether there is knowledge, it will vanish away. For we know in part and we prophesy in part. But when that which is perfect has come, then that which is in part will be done away.

When I was a child, I spoke as a child, I understood as a child, I thought as a child; but when I became a man, I put away childish things. For now we see in a mirror dimly, but then face to face. Now I know in part, but then I shall know just as I also am known.

And now abide faith, hope, love, these three;
but the greatest of these is love.
1 Corinthians 13:8–13

Change is a fact of life; we all live with it constantly. Sometimes it seems to happen overnight, as when a familiar landmark is demolished for a new construction project. More often it comes slowly and gradually, as the gentle fade in the colour of our favourite shirt. Whatever the case, change always comes. We want stability in the midst of the variations and modifications of life. We seek for things that are trusty and dependable—consistent—to give us familiar sources of strength to face change. Paul deals with this basic need in our passage, that the grace of love remains among the variations of life.

Instability was very much present in the Corinthian church: they acted like children, seeking their own glory and forgetting others, pushing and shoving their way to prominence, all the while neglecting the most basic, and most permanent of truths, love. With change all around, the Christian must look to the enduring—the permanent, the unshakeable—found in the grace of love. The apostle seems to say, "Corinthians! Take your eyes off yourselves, and learn to long for the grace of love, because love never fails."

Love Never Fails

After listing fifteen aspects, positive and negative, of love's actions, Paul concludes with this grand statement. His intent is to summarize and emphasize the supreme value of love. But what does he mean?

The word used in 13:8 has the sense of to "fall down; collapse; be ruined; be destroyed". Something that never fails always remains the same by its nature. In Luke 16:17, we find very similar language: "It is easier for heaven and earth to pass away than for one tittle of the law to fail." Here, the Lord Jesus speaks of the law of God, asserting that it stands eternal. In contrast with heaven and earth, places that seem permanent but will not endure, God's law in its entirety lasts for ever. Not even the smallest part of one of the letters used to write the law can fail. The moral standards of a holy God frame his law, and it is unchangeable. As God himself is immutable, so also is the transcript of his character. It cannot be set aside nor altered—it cannot fail. In 1 Corinthians 13:8, Paul teaches us that love takes on this same quality. Do you know why?

The reason is really simple: love reflects the nature of God. For the same reason that the law cannot fail, love cannot; it is a moral quality belonging to God, an aspect of his very being.

There are two things we must consider and remember:

(1) God is love

These words, found in 1 John 4:16, are simple and yet profound. Our God, the holy, eternal, triune Lord of heaven and earth, in the very essence of his being, is love. Love is not a creation, or a created entity, but an eternal moral quality, a reality that is part of what God is. Love is, because God is, and every definition of love must take account of the relationship between God and love.

Paul can say, "Love never fails" (13:8), because God never fails. He is immutable, unchangeable, and so long as he is, there will be true, holy love. This is really tremendous! God is love, and, as Paul writes, he describes to us the character of love as it shines forth from God. *He* is longsuffering and kind; *he* expresses all of the perfections of true love, and as we live in these ways, we shine forth God's love. We reflect the beauty and brilliance of his wonderful love.

But even more importantly, we must consider our second point.

(2) Jesus Christ is the perfect embodiment of this love in humanity

The preceding paragraph (13:4–7) could be a description of the life and ministry of our Lord Jesus Christ. His name could be inserted into each of the phrases found here, and they would all be true. We must contemplate Jesus, the true God-man. In the words of Chapter 8 of the Second London Baptist Confession:

> The Son of God, the second Person in the Holy Trinity, being very and eternal God, the brightness of the Fathers glory, of one substance and equal with him: who made the World, who

> upholdeth and governeth all things he hath made: did when the fullness of time was come take unto him man's nature, with all the Essential properties, and common infirmities thereof, yet without sin: being conceived by the Holy Spirit in the Womb of the Virgin Mary, the Holy Spirit coming down upon her, and the power of the most High overshadowing her, and so was made of a Woman, of the Tribe of Judah, of the Seed of Abraham, and David according to the Scriptures: So that two whole, perfect, and distinct natures, were inseparably joined together in one Person: without conversion, composition, or confusion: which Person is very God, and very Man; yet one Christ, the only Mediator between God and Man. (2LCF 8.2)

He is truly God, and yet truly man. The second person of the holy Trinity stooped to unite his deity with true humanity and lived among humans. In doing this, he lived before men and women a perfect life of unqualified love, in the power of the Holy Spirit. Paul is able to point to the firm stability of human love, because of Christ.

Love never fails, because God is love, and because Jesus Christ is love. The Corinthians must look away from themselves to God in Christ, for only here is the true demonstration of love.

Gifts Are Temporary

We must take note of how Paul illustrates the point; he does so by zeroing in on two problem areas in their church, using them as illustrations of his point. In verses 8–10, the apostle addresses one of the great problem issues within the Corinthian assembly. In many ways, the believers in this church were enamoured with the status attached to certain spiritual gifts, desiring the showiest ones. In chapter 14, much of the argument revolves around the abuse of these things. When we read Paul's words, we get the impression that their meetings resembled a "free-for-all", an out-of-control, chaotic, disorderly gathering hardly recognizable as worship. As the exercise of gifts was considered the height of spirituality, the Corinthians fought to show their advanced status in the use of such gifts. The result was a church that more resembled a busy marketplace than a house of God. Paul found it necessary to give them detailed instructions to bring order out of their chaos.

The wise apostle seeks to show these Christians that the gifts—even the best of them—are only temporary. Indeed, they serve a purpose for a time, but they do not last beyond their appointed usefulness. Gifts *are* good, as is clearly stated in 1 Corinthians 14:1, and they serve a purpose; but to be those who lose sight of love, and become attached to gifts, is to be like the man who is so taken up with his work that he neglects his family. His job is important and has a rightful place to serve and provide, but not to the point of disrupting the function of his family.

Gifts are good, but love never fails. Our gifts are limited—we know in part, we prophesy in part—but not so love. It carries on, it grows, it fills us and moulds us to be like the Saviour. Grace, especially love, is far superior to gift.

Maturity Is Essential

Earlier in this letter, Paul addressed the childish behaviour of the Corinthians. Their divisive spirit was more fitting of young "babes" than mature Christians (1 Cor. 3:1–2). While he thinks of them as his "beloved children", (4:14), he recognizes that their actions and understanding can be childish (14:20). In every case, the lesson is the same: child-like behaviour must be left behind on the way to maturity. In 13:11–12, the idea is exactly the same. In the first place, the apostle uses his own experience as an illustration. His young years were essentially the same as everyone else's. Yet every adult ought to know that there is an obvious difference between the behaviour of a child and a man; or at least there should be.

A child is often selfish and self-centred. He speaks often of himself, tries to understand life through his own experiences, reasons in simplistic fashions. Parents recognize these traits and know that they must help their children to grow out of these patterns. What is expected of a teenager is far different from a six-year-old. As the young person grows, it is anticipated that he or she will reflect a growing understanding of the adult world and will be able to take a place there. Maturity is the result of progressive, incremental change.

The Corinthians were childlike, rather than mature, in their acts. While they boasted in their gifts, promoting themselves as the most spiritual, their actions demonstrated that they were more like self-centred children than mature, responsible adults. The time has come to put away these acts and put on love.

Beyond this, Paul's present experience evidences the importance of love. Even now, he knows that he has not achieved perfection in holiness or knowledge, and must press on, seeking to grow in love in the midst of the changes of life, until the day when he will enter the world of love, and see his Saviour face to face. This is the love that never fails, for it provides the never-failing moral vigour that shows forth the glory of God.

Love never fails, because it cannot change. It is an aspect of God's eternal character, which he graciously allows us to share for ever, in his world of love. Paul would have us seek the permanent and eternal, in the midst of the flux of the temporal.

Friend, what is the priority in your life? To what are you giving your time and effort? What do your children see you pursue as the most fulfilling and satisfying thing in life? Is it the grace of love? Too often we fall prey to the attractive and outward and showy, hoping to gain honour and recognition. But does it last? Remember what Jesus said about those who sought the praises of men: "They have their reward" (Matt. 6:2).

Love never fails. Do you seek the enduring grace of love? How is the Word of God changing you? What effect does it have on your family relationships? On your church fellowships? On your acquaintances in the world? Do you see the never-failing grace of love growing in your heart?

More pointedly, if we would feel the weight of Paul's teaching, we should try a little heart-searching exercise: read 1 Corinthians 13:4–7 and replace the word "love" with your name. Are these things true of you? Paul is not simply creating a beautiful hymn to love; he is exhorting us to love. Read what the apostle says, apply it to yourself, and always remember that love never fails. Cry out for the Spirit's help, that you might see this grace grow and dominate your life.

What is our motivation to love? Surely it is the gospel itself. John said it well: "In this is love, not that we loved God, but that He loved us and sent His Son to be the propitiation for our sins. Beloved, if God so loved us, we also ought to love one another" (1 John 4:10–11). Here is all we need: forgiveness of sins, and God-centred motivation to grow. Will you?

May God help us to grow in the grace of the love that never fails.

Chapter 11
PURSUE LOVE

And now abide faith, hope, love, these three;
but the greatest of these is love.
Pursue love…
1 Corinthians 13:13–14:1

How does one grow in grace? The Bible teaches us that our progress must always be rooted in the gracious work done for us by God in Christ. The source of power for our advance does not bubble up from within; rather, it is drawn from the well-spring of life—the Holy Spirit.

As we walk, dependant on the Holy Spirit, it is our task to seek and strive for growth. True Christianity is working Christianity—one that works not for justification, but in grateful response to the gracious work done by divine power. We must battle against sin and take up the way of holiness. In every aspect of our lives, whether in the war with indwelling corruption or in the increase of grace, we are called to seek progress. We cannot expect to conquer any sin until we aim at killing every sin; and we will not grow in any area of grace unless we seek after every area of grace.

This is Paul's theme in 1 Corinthians 13:13–14:1—gifts are temporary, but grace abides. Faith, hope, and love are foundational, but love is the greatest of all, and we are to pursue it relentlessly.

Graces Grow Together

The graces of Christianity are mutually dependent. Consider how verse 13 repeats the theme of verse 7, "Love believes all things, hopes all things." Faith, hope, and love are entwined in mutual expression and development. Love does not grow alone in us, but rather blossoms and bears fruit along with these other graces. The cross-pollination brings an abundance at harvest time.

Faith, hope, and love seem to have been regarded as a trio of the most elemental graces. One scholar asserts that the words "these three" was a familiar phrase used to describe them.[31] In the Scriptures, they are frequently tied together.

Take note of the following passages:[32]

> For we through the Spirit eagerly wait for the hope of righteousness by faith. For in Christ Jesus neither circumcision nor uncircumcision avails anything, but faith working through love. (Gal. 5:5–6)

> We give thanks to the God and Father of our Lord Jesus Christ, praying always for you, since we heard of your faith in Christ Jesus and of your love for all the saints; because of the hope which is laid up for you in heaven… (Col. 1:3–5)

> We give thanks to God always for you all, making mention of you in our prayers, remembering without ceasing your work of faith, labour of love, and patience of hope in our Lord Jesus Christ… (1 Thess. 1:2–3)

---

31 Fee, *1 Corinthians*, 650, n. 57.

32 See also Romans 5:1–5; Ephesians 4:2–5; 1 Peter 1:3–8.

> But let us who are of the day be sober, putting on the breastplate of faith and love, and as a helmet the hope of salvation. (1 Thess. 5:8)

> For God is not unjust to forget your work and labour of love which you have shown toward His name … And we desire that each one of you show the same diligence to the full assurance of hope until the end, that you do not become sluggish, but imitate those who through faith and patience inherit the promises. (Heb. 6:10–12)

> Let us draw near with a true heart in full assurance of faith, having our hearts sprinkled from an evil conscience and our bodies washed with pure water. Let us hold fast the confession of our hope without wavering, for He who promised is faithful. And let us consider one another in order to stir up love and good works. (Heb. 10:22–24)

In this last passage in Hebrews, the graces are detailed with relation to the Christian life, and this helps us to define them. Based on the finished work of Christ (10:19–21), faith is the means of drawing near to God as his cleansed and forgiven children; hope is confident certainty, based on the nature of the promises and their author, God himself; and love is the demonstration of good will and good deeds in the regular assembly of Christ's people (see 10:25).

In all of these texts we see how these graces are interrelated. Could you imagine a Christian without any of these? With faith but no hope, hope but no love, love but no faith? Each of them is foundational and essential to the Christian life, and the writers indicate this. But even recognizing this truth, love is greater. Do you know why?

In 1 Corinthians 13:13, we are given the reason. Paul begins his statement with the words "and now". He turns our attention to the present circumstances of life, between the two advents of Christ. It is in this interim period—that is, after the events of Christ's life, death, resurrection, and ascension, after the descent of the Spirit at Pentecost, but before Christ returns to establish his eternal kingdom —that these three foundational graces abide. They are the means by which we lay hold of God, but it will not always be so.

Faith is a grace for this present age. The apostle says in 2 Corinthians 5:7: "For we walk by faith, not by sight." Faith is the instrument by which we *now* lay hold of what we cannot see. This is what Hebrews 11:1 teaches us: "Now faith is the substance of things hoped for, the evidence of things not seen." Faith is not a grace for eternity; it is a gift for us now. When we see him face to face, we shall "know just as [we] also [are] known" (1 Cor. 13:12). There will come a time when faith is no longer necessary.

Similarly, hope is also for the present age. In Romans 8:24, the apostle says, "hope that is seen is not hope." Hope is the confident assurance that the promises of God will be fulfilled, a certainty that God will do what he has said. But when that is realized, it is no longer hope; it is reality. Hope is not a grace for eternity, it is a privilege we enjoy now. There will come a time when hope is no longer necessary.

Not so with love. Jonathan Edwards penned an exposition of 1 Corinthians 13 and titled his final chapter of that book "Heaven, a world of love". The heavenly kingdom will be full of never-dying love.

Likewise, Paul uses the strongest language to make this point:

> For I am persuaded that neither death nor life, nor angels nor principalities nor powers, nor things present nor things to come, nor height nor depth, nor any other created thing, shall

> be able to separate us from the love of God which is in Christ Jesus our Lord. (Rom. 8:38–39)

Why is this? Because God is love. As we have stated already, it is an aspect of his moral character, and thus lasts throughout all of eternity. Faith and hope are essential for us now, but even more so is love, for we will spend eternity in a world of love. And this is why Paul follows these words with the simple command, "Pursue love" (1 Cor. 14:1).

The Pursuit of Love

After setting before us the beauties of this grace, the apostle commands us to take up, with single-minded devotion, the increase of love in our lives. The word "pursue" implies an aggressively dedicated aspiration. When he speaks of his determination to know Christ, in Philippians 3: 14, he uses the same word: "I press toward the goal for the prize of the upward call of God in Christ Jesus." Similarly, peace is to be pursued with vigour (Rom. 14:19), just as good works should be (1 Thess. 5:15). It is used to describe someone driven with a purpose in order to reach a goal. A world-class athlete, or a talented musician, or even a man greedy for money or power, will marshal all of his resources to achieve his goal. The athlete seeks the champion's prize; the musician desires perfection in performance; the greedy man aims to accumulate wealth. The dedication to these tasks can be astounding. Olympic athletes develop training regimens for every muscle they use in competition; musicians spend hours learning the technical aspects of their instrument. Paul says that Christians are to strive for this kind of devotion to the increase of love, that this should be our attitude towards the love described in 1 Corinthians 13:4–7.

Why is this important? The words of 1 Corinthians 13:8 should ring in our ears: "Love never fails." After all is said and done, love remains. What else should we give ourselves to? For all of their desire to excel, athletes and musicians dedicate themselves to the wrong thing. I am not saying that there is no benefit in winning the prize, nor in giving a virtuoso performance. But without love (13:1–3), these things are nothing. On judgement day, the pursuit of even the best things offered by the world will be empty. Everything will be gone, including athletic glory or musical renown. Not so with love, for those who truly seek it will find it, and they will possess it for ever. It is a pursuit richly rewarded in the grace of God.

Do you pursue love? Upon what do you set your mind and affection? All of us pursue something, perhaps not as great a thing as others, but we pursue them nonetheless. We want comfort, happiness, security, respect, power. All of these things are substitutes for grace, and for the greatest grace, love. The late Francis Schaeffer spoke of our generation in the West as consumed with two dubious values, personal peace and affluence. So long as things are going well for us, and we have enough for the little luxuries of life, then nothing else matters. This is the devil's lie.

Let us think of these three graces again. Right now, faith is one of the central graces of Christianity, and we must exercise it so that it is strong. This was especially appropriate for the Corinthians. Think about chapter 1 of this epistle. Paul said that "The message of the cross is foolishness to those who are perishing, but to us who are being saved it is the power of God" (1:18). Faith lays hold of Christ and his cross, even in the face of great unbelief. It rests on and relies on him; it seeks him and follows him and loves him. The Corinthians needed faith, and so do we. Are you exercising your faith in Christ?

Right now, hope is one of the central graces of Christianity. It has everything to do with our faith. It is the confident assurance that God's promises will be true, in every way that he intends. Since the Corinthians had misunderstood the kingdom of God, hope was essential for them. They lived as if the kingdom had come in its fulness, as if they were kings, and they were "puffed up" with pride. Their understanding of the Christian life was seriously flawed. Hope causes us to recognize the difference between this present evil age and the perfect age to come, teaching us not to be settled here, but to persevere, pressing into the eternal kingdom. Are you exercising hope?

Love is a grace for now, and for ever. It is the most beautiful of graces expressed now, the product of the Spirit's work within us, and it is preparation for our future life in the presence of the One who is love.

Do you love? Will you, by the help of the Holy Spirit, because of union with Christ in the gospel, pursue it?

May God help all of us to show forth the love of Jesus Christ in our lives. Amen.

Chapter 12
TRUE LOVE

But God demonstrates His own love toward us,
in that while we were still sinners, Christ died for us.
Romans 5:8

Before we leave our study, there is one more thing that must be said. In the first chapter, we noticed that love must be understood in terms of the law and the gospel. When viewed as law, love is a commandment that must be obeyed. It is about righteous deeds and pure motivations. In this sense, love is unattainable and discouraging. As we cannot meet its lofty standard, and we are revealed as *sinners*. Love condemns us.

Thankfully, this is not all that Scripture says about love. It is also gospel. Love is an action confirmed to us by God, in and through his Son Jesus Christ. The Bible is full of this *gospel* truth. I don't hesitate for a moment in saying that it is the great central truth of the Bible.

Consider the Old Testament, a book of promise and anticipation. It looks forward to the day when Messiah would come to fulfil all of God's promises. Wherever we read in the Old Testament scriptures, they point us to the future, with a powerful longing and expectation. With growing clarity, God revealed his plan and purpose of salvation for his people. When Adam stood next to Eve and listened to the Lord pronounce a curse upon the serpent, did they marvel at God's mercy in the promise of a "seed" who would crush the serpent's head (Gen. 3:15)? When Moses wrote about a great prophet who was to come (Deut. 18:15, 18); when David contemplated the glory of the LORD who spoke to his Lord (Ps. 110—the most frequently quoted psalm in the New Testament); and Isaiah sang of the Suffering Servant (Isa. 42; 49; 50; 52–53), did their hearts leap at God's promise?

Peter seems to think so when he says in 1 Peter 1:10–12:

> Of this salvation the prophets have inquired and searched carefully, who prophesied of the grace that would come to you, searching what, or what manner of time, the Spirit of Christ who was in them was indicating when He testified beforehand the sufferings of Christ and the glories that would follow. To them it was revealed that, not to themselves, but to us they were ministering the things which now have been reported to you through those who have preached the gospel to you by the Holy Spirit sent from heaven—things which angels desire to look into.

If the Old Testament is about promise, the New Testament is about fulfilment. It begins with the birth of the One promised so long before, and tells of his life, death, resurrection, and ascension into heaven. In the fulness of time, God sent his Son (Gal. 4:4), and his name is Jesus Christ. It shows how the promises given over millennia to the saints came to pass in history. God was true to his words. When Mark starts his Gospel with the words, "The beginning of the gospel of Jesus Christ", it is a momentous thing. The time has come—God's promises are coming to fruition.

Think about this for a moment. Why did God promise these things? We should say, "It was because of his love." The apostle John states this plainly: "God is love" (1 John 4:8, 16). The law condemns us. It shows us our sin. It reveals the depth of our wickedness and proves to us that we cannot satisfy the demands of God's righteousness. When love is considered as law, it too convicts us. But when we see God's love in action in Jesus Christ, it becomes gospel. It tells us that there is another who has obeyed the law on our behalf, and who died to take our punishment. Jesus Christ loved perfectly—he obeyed its precepts without fail, and then he gave himself to die in order to satisfy its demand for justice. Love is both law and gospel. It demands perfect obedience, and provides a remedy for our failure, in Christ!

It was the apostle Paul who said,

> For when we were still without strength, in due time Christ died for the ungodly. For scarcely for a righteous man will one die; yet perhaps for a good man someone would even dare to die. But God demonstrates His own love toward us, in that while we were still sinners, Christ died for us. (Rom. 5:6–8)

Do you believe in Jesus Christ? Are you seeking to practise love, hoping that you will do it well enough to merit God's favour? I must tell you that you will fail. But God's love, revealed to us in his beloved Son, in his life, death and resurrection, will cause to you succeed for ever. Not on the basis of what you have done—but in and through Jesus Christ. Trust him today.

For many of us, a book about love may be discouraging, but that is because the law is always discouraging. It teaches us what we cannot do. We believers must remember two complementary truths: on the one hand, God promises forgiveness when we confess our sins (1 John 1:9). If you are discouraged by your lack of love, confess your sin to God, and receive his forgiveness. On the other hand, because he has loved you in Christ, you may now serve him with joy and with true love. "In this is love, not that we loved God, but that He loved us and sent His Son *to be* the propitiation for our sins. Beloved, if God so loved us, we also ought to love one another" (1 John 4:10–11). "And now abide faith, hope, love, these three; but the greatest of these is love." (1 Cor. 13: 13)

May God help us to abide in his love.

Bibliography

Barclay, William. *The Letters to the Corinthians: New Daily Study Bible.* Philadelphia, Westminster Press, 1956.

Bertram, Robert Aitkin, ed. *A Homiletic Encyclopaedia Of Illustrations in Theology and Morals.* New York: Funk & Wagnalls, 1889.

Blaiklock, E. M.. *The Acts of the Apostles: An Historical Commentary.* Grand Rapids: Eerdmans, 1959.

Carson, D. A.. *Showing the Spirit: A Theological Exposition of 1 Corinthians 12–14.* Grand Rapids: Baker, 1987.

Fee, Gordon. *The First Epistle to the Corinthians: The New International Commentary on the New Testament.* Grand Rapids: Eerdmans, 1987.

Ferguson, Sinclair. "The Reformed View." In *Christian Spirituality: Five Views of Sanctification*, edited by Donald L. Alexander, 47–76. Downers Grove: InterVarsity, 1988.

MacArthur, John. *1 Corinthians.* Vol. 17 of *MacArthur New Testament Commentary.* Chicago: Moody Press, 1984.

Smedes, Lewis. *Love Within Limits: Realizing Selfless Love in a Selfish World.* Grand Rapids: Eerdmans, 1978.

Westcott, B. F.. *The Epistles of St John: The Greek Text with Notes and Essays.* Grand Rapids: Eerdmans, 1966.